SHAKESPEARE'S IMPACT ON HIS CONTEMPORARIES

SHAKESPEARE'S IMPACT ON HIS CONTEMPORARIES

E. A. J. Honigmann

BARNES & NOBLE BOOKS
TOTOWA, NEW JERSEY

First published in the USA 1982 by
BARNES & NOBLE BOOKS
81 Adams Drive, Totowa,
New Jersey, 07512

ISBN 0-389-20108-1

Printed in Hong Kong

822.33

DH757sha

Library of Congress Cataloging in Publication Data

Honigmann, E. A. J.
Shakespeare's impact on his contemporaries.

Includes index.
1. Shakespeare, William, 1564–1616—Contemporaries.
2. Shakespeare, William, 1564–1616—Influence.
3. English literature—Early modern, 1500–1700—History
and criticism. 4. Dramatists, English—Early modern,
1500–1700—Biography. I. Title.
PR2911.H56   1982   822.3′ 3   81–17591
ISBN 0–389–20108–1   AACR2

For Peter Alexander
(1894−1969)

Contents

Preface

'He was not of an age, but for all time.' Looking back across almost four centuries, we have to admit that Jonson judged correctly: Shakespeare's importance to posterity cannot be disputed. But what of Shakespeare's impact on his contemporaries? It has been said that he was 'rated at something like his true value by most persons of taste and judgement', and also that there is 'little or no direct evidence that the major dramatists thought of him as a master'. The facts, one might suppose, having been long available in allusion books and biographies, surely cannot support two such contradictory views. Pursue the 'facts', however, and you discover a strange story of misunderstanding or incompetence: crucial passages from the records have been misread, or have been ignored because they clashed with preconceived ideas. A careful re-examination of the records will compel us to revise current thinking about the dramatist's contemporary impact in many unexpected ways, throwing new light on his personality, his development as a writer, his influence on other writers, and his response to criticism. This book is a beginning. It cannot claim to be a rounded biography, since it proceeds selectively, but it offers a new 'Shakespeare', and a new understanding of his achievement.

One reason for the misreading of early records must be mentioned immediately. It is that they have been studied in allusion books or biographies, torn from their context. '*Sweet* Swan of Avon' and '*gentle* Shakespeare' are examples: Jonson's epithets conjure up a mild-mannered, sweet-tempered poet – a 'soft' Shakespeare who is all too familiar. Here the context includes Jonson's long-standing relationship with Shakespeare, the occasion of his commemorative poem of 1623, the conventions of elegy, the rhetoric of praise; and to disregard the context is to run the risk of sentimentalising. The 'Elizabethan' context of the early records is a theme to which I return repeatedly, since I believe that imperfect knowledge of the by-ways of Elizabethan life and letters has too often caused confusion. Wherever possible I have consulted the original documents, and often I quote extracts that will not be recognised in their present form. (The authors of standard works tend to copy the same 'allusions' verbatim from one another, forgetting that the force of an

ix

allusion may be affected by the sentences that precede or follow it, or by the tone or argument of the text as a whole.) For the reader's convenience – and my own – I do, however, cite some of these contemporary witnesses from standard works, such as E. K. Chambers's *William Shakespeare* (2 vols, 1930), in cases where 'contextual' difficulties do not arise.

Although Anthony Burgess, Edward Bond and others have tried to present Shakespeare the Man in new ways, the more 'official' commentators cling to an established formula, and usually paint the same pleasant picture. I do not recollect any survey of the less flattering evidence, which survives in some quantity (though not in modern biographies, where crucial witnesses sometimes disappear silently, or are not given their full say). In starting with this, the less familiar view of Shakespeare the Man, I hope to show that the traditional picture is incomplete. As will be seen, while we may be suspicious of some of the witnesses against Shakespeare, once we place them in their context the cumulative weight of their evidence is considerable. We may not like the new Shakespeare as much as the old sentimental model, but at least it can be said that he becomes a more credible human being.

Three of the remaining chapters (2, 5 and 6) deal, one way or another, with Shakespeare's impact on his contemporaries as a writer. What did they like in the plays? And dislike? Why did the demand for printed plays begin so late? We read often enough that without an understanding audience Shakespeare would never have written the plays – but is it really so? My story stops in 1623, with the publication of the first Folio, even though informed contemporaries lived on for years and we cannot wholly ignore their later statements. In these three chapters, I now find to my surprise, Ben Jonson plays almost as large a part as Shakespeare. To my surprise – for I did not plan it that way, nor did I realise that some of Jonson's most fretful criticisms of his great rival had not yet been identified. Students of Jonson the Man who are not greatly interested in Shakespeare, if such there be, may also think these chapters revealing.

Two central chapters of this book are concerned with the dating of Shakespeare's first plays. I have ignored the chronology of the later plays, having little to add to the textbooks; but the textbooks are wrong, I believe, in their dates for the early plays, and in what they tell us about Shakespeare's first impact on the London literary scene, and must be challenged. My argument turns on the relationship of the two King John plays, one by Shakespeare and the other anonymous, a tale of a tub that fascinated me from 1948 to 1954, and that I then abandoned (as Swift might have said) to divert the whales. The whales sported happily and spouted mightily, but solved no problems, Returning now to *King John* after a quarter of a century I am particularly conscious of my debt to three brilliant teachers, Peter Alexander, J. C. Maxwell and F. P. Wilson, who advised me long ago: I can only hope that, had they lived, they would have given their approval not only to a thesis presented in 1950 but also to its belated afterbirth.

It is also a pleasure to acknowledge more recent debts. I am grateful to the University of Newcastle upon Tyne for a term's study-leave, which gave me the leisure to write this book; to Kathleen O'Rawe, Kay Moore and Barbara Kugler, who helped to type it; to Mr A. D. Robinson, who suggested several corrections and improvements; and particularly to my wife, who checked the typescript and once again helped me with proof-reading. Dr R. L. Smallwood, the editor of one of the most careful editions of *King John*, generously found time to read through my manuscript and made many suggestions: he has his own views about some of the issues that I discuss, but I have benefited greatly from his perceptive criticism.

September 1980   E. A. J. H.

List of Abbreviations

The customary abbreviations are employed for Shakespeare's plays, and for periodicals. Works frequently referred to are quoted by short titles only: their full titles will be found in the list below.

Allusion-Book. *The Shakspere Allusion-Book: A Collection of Allusions to Shakspere from 1591 to 1700,* edited by John Munro (1909), re-issued with a Preface by Sir Edmund Chambers (2 vols, 1932).

Apocrypha. *The Shakespeare Apocrypha,* edited by C. F. Tucker Brooke (Oxford, 1918).

Arber. *Transcript of the Registers of the Company of Stationers, 1554–1640,* edited by E. Arber (5 vols, 1875–94).

Bentley, *Profession of Dramatist. The Profession of Dramatist in Shakespeare's Time 1590–1642,* by G. E. Bentley (Princeton, 1971).

Bentley, *Shakespeare & Jonson. Shakespeare & Jonson Their Reputations in the Seventeenth Century Compared,* by G. E. Bentley (2 vols, Chicago, 1945).

Dryden, *Essays. Essays of John Dryden,* edited by W. P. Ker (2 vols, Oxford, 1900).

EKC. William Shakespeare A Study of Facts and Problems, by E. K. Chambers (2 vols, Oxford, 1930).

EKC, ES. The Elizabethan Stage, by E. K. Chambers (4 vols, Oxford, 1923).

GWW. Robert Greene, *Groats-Worth of Witte* (1592) (quoted from *Elizabethan and Jacobean Quartos,* edited by G. B. Harrison Edinburgh, 1966).

Harvey, *Works. The Works of Gabriel Harvey,* edited by A. B. Grosart (3 vols, privately printed, 1884).

Jonson. *Ben Jonson,* edited by C. H. Herford and Percy and Evelyn Simpson (11 vols, Oxford, 1925–52).

Muir, *Sources. The Sources of Shakespeare's Plays,* by Kenneth Muir (1977).

Nashe, *Works. The Works of Thomas Nashe,* edited by R. B. McKerrow (5 vols, Oxford, 1958 (reprinted by F. P. Wilson)).

OED.   The Oxford English Dictionary, edited by James A. H. Murray *et al* (13 vols, Oxford, 1933).
Schoenbaum, *Life.   William Shakespeare A Documentary Life,* by S. Schoenbaum (Oxford, 1975).
SR.   See Arber.
TR.   Anon., The Troublesome Raigne of Iohn King of England (2 vols 1591: quoted from G. Bullough, *Narrative and Dramatic Sources of Shakespeare* (8 vols, 1957 etc.), vol. IV (1962)).

Modernised quotations from Shakespeare, and line-references, are taken from Peter Alexander's *William Shakespeare, The Complete Works* (Collins, 1951).

Old-spelling quotations from Elizabethan texts are from the first editions. In a few cases (usually indicated by footnotes) they are taken from EKC, or from modern editions. Black-letter texts are printed as roman; and some texts in italics have also been converted to roman. I have expanded contractions, and have lowered letters printed superior. Square brackets in quotations indicate my insertions in the text.

1
The Man

(I) A 'WASPISH LITTLE WORME'

Every biography of Shakespeare quotes Greene's[1] death-bed attack upon 'an absolute *Iohannes fac totum*' who 'is in his owne conceit the onely Shake-scene in a countrey', the earliest surviving indication that the young man from Stratford had now (September 1592) won a place for himself in the literary world of London: yet no biographer appears to have noticed that Greene had more to say about his rival in the same pamphlet. This is because, writing his autobiography in a curiously oblique way, Greene teases the reader by sliding from romance to private reminiscence to fable, from third to first person and back to third. Once his circling technique is understood, however, it becomes difficult to resist the conclusion that he proceeded from the only Shake-scene in a country to the fable of the grasshopper and the ant in order to pillory Shakespeare as the ant – a 'waspish little worme'.

Greene's *Groats-Worth of Witte* (hereafter *GWW*) begins as the story of Roberto, 'a Scholler, and maried to a proper Gentlewoman', whose father, a usurer, bequeathes to him a groat, 'to buy a groats-worth of wit', leaving his fortune to another son, Lucanio. To revenge himself, Roberto conspires with the courtesan Lamilia to cheat Lucanio of his money. She reveals the plot and Roberto, cast adrift, is befriended by a rich actor, who persuades him to write plays. He is soon 'famozed for an Arch-plaimaking-poet', earns much and spends much, and finally lies on his death-bed 'in extreame pouerty . . . hauing but one groat left'. At this point Greene interrupts what had appeared to be a typical moralising romance of the 1580s –

Heere (Gentlemen) breake I off *Robertoes* speach; whose life in most parts agreeing with mine, found one selfe punishment as I haue doone. Heereafter suppose me the saide *Roberto* . . .

1

After exhorting the gentlemen who read *GWW* to learn from this example, Greene adds a letter – 'To those Gentlemen his Quondam acquaintance, that spend their wits in making plaies, R. G. wisheth a better exercise, and wisdome to preuent his extremities.' He addresses three dramatists, usually thought to be Marlowe, Nashe and Peele, then launches into the famous sentences about Shakespeare.

> Base minded men all three of you, if by my miserie you be not warnd: for vnto none of you (like mee) sought those burres to cleaue: those Puppets (I meane) that spake from our mouths, those Anticks garnisht in our colours. Is it not strange, that I, to whom they all haue beene beholding: is it not like that you, to whome they all haue beene beholding, shall (were yee in that case as I am now) bee both at once of them forsaken? Yes trust them not: for there is an vpstart Crow, beautified with our feathers, that with his *Tygers hart wrapt in a Players hyde*, supposes he is as well able to bombast out a blanke verse as the best of you: and beeing an absolute *Iohannes fac totum*, is in his owne conceit the onely Shake-scene in a countrey. O that I might intreat your rare wits to be imploied in more profitable courses: & let those Apes imitate your past excellence, and neuer more acquaint them with your admired inuentions. I knowe the best husband of you all will neuer proue an Vsurer, and the kindest of them all will neuer proue a kind nurse . . .

The letter concludes with advice given before – 'Trust not then (I beseech ye) to such weake staies: for they are as changeable in minde, as in many attyres'. Thereupon Greene switches abruptly to the ant and the grasshopper, a passage that must be quoted in full.

> Now to all men I bid farewel in like sort, with this conceited Fable of that olde Comedian *Aesope.*

> An Ant and a Grashopper walking together on a Greene, the one carelesly skipping, the other carefully prying what winters prouision was scattered in the way: the Grashopper scorning (as wantons will) this needlesse thrift (as hee tearmed it) reprooued him thus:

> *The greedy miser thirsteth still for gaine,*
> *His thrift is theft, his weale works others woe:*
> *That foole is fond which will in caues remaine,*
> *VVhen mongst faire sweets he may at pleasure goe.*

To this the Ant perceiuing the Grashoppers meaning, quickly replyde:

The thriftie husband spares what vnthrift spends,
His thrift no theft, for dangers to prouide:
Trust to thy selfe, small hope in want yeeld friends,
A caue is better than the deserts wide.

In short time these two parted, the one to his pleasure, the other to his labour. Anon Haruest grew on, and reft from the Grashopper his woonted moysture. Then weakly skipt hee to the medowes brinks: where till fell winter he abode. But storms continually powring, hee went for succour to the Ant his olde acquaintance, to whom hee had scarce discouered his estate, but the waspish little worme made this reply,

Packe hence (quoth he) thou idle lazie worme,
My house doth harbor no vnthriftie mates:
Thou scorndst to toile, & now thou feelst the storme,
And starust for food while I am fed with cates.
 Vse no intreats, I will relentlesse rest,
 For toyling labour hates an idle guest.

The Grashopper foodlesse, helplesse and strengthles, got into the next brooke, and in the yeelding sand digde for himselfe a pit: by which hee likewise ingrau'de this Epitaph,

When Springs greene prime arrayd me with delight,
And euery power with youthful vigor fild,
Gaue strength on worke what euer fancie wild:
I neuer feard the force of winters spight.

When first I saw the sunne the day begin,
And dry the Mornings tears from hearbs and grasse;
I little thought his chearefull light would passe,
Till vgly night with darknes enterd in.
 And then day lost I mournd, spring past I wayld,
 But neither teares for this or that auailde.

Then too too late I praisd the Emmets paine,
That sought in spring a harbor gainst the heate:
And in the haruest gathered winters meat,
Preuenting famine, frosts, and stormy raine.

My wretched end may warn Greene springing youth
To vse delights, as toyes that will deceiue,
And scorne the world before the world them leaue:

For all worlds trust, is ruine without ruth.
Then blest are they that like the toyling Ant,
Prouide in time gainst winters wofull want.

With this the Grashopper yeelding to the wethers extremit, died com-
fortles without remedy. Like him my selfe: like me, shall all that trust
to friends or times inconstancie. Now faint I of my last infirmity, be-
seeching them that shall burie my bodie, to publish this last farewell
written with my wretched hand.

Just as Roberto had turned into Robert Greene, the grasshopper is also
later identified as the author ('Like him my selfe'), a point that was
gleefully seized upon by Gabriel Harvey ('the Grashopper enraged, would
bee no lesse then a greene Dragon'[2]). And the fable reverts to Greene's
earlier complaints in obsessively echoing his earlier warning – 'trust them
not': (1) 'Yes, trust them not: for there is an vpstart Crow'; (2) 'Trust
not then ... to such weake staies'; (3) 'Trust to thy selfe, small hope in
want yeeld friends'; (4) 'Like me, shall all that trust to friends ...'. The
fable, therefore, though apparently quite casually tagged on after the
letter, develops the charges contained in the letter. But the target is not
only the foolishness of grasshopper lives, as in Aesop's fable: Greene also
manages to present the sensible ant in a new light. Compare John Prime,
in a sermon of 1588: 'And this is true wisedome indeede ... with the
wise Emite in sommer to lay vp for the winter following'.[3] Or Caxton's
version of Aesop:

It is good to purueye hym self in the somer season of suche thynges /
wherof he shalle myster [need] and haue nede in wynter season / As
thow mayst see by this present fable / Of the sygalle / whiche in the
wynter tyme went and demaunded of the ant somme of her Corne for
to ete / And thenne the Ant sayd to the sygall / what hast thow done
al the somer last passed / And the sygalle ansuerd / I haue songe / And
after sayd the ante to her / Of my corne shalt not thou none haue /
And yf thow hast songe alle the somer / daunse now in wynter / And
therfore there is one tyme for to doo some labour and werk / And one
tyme for to haue rest / For he that werketh not ne doth no good / shal
haue ofte at his teeth grete cold and lacke at his nede / [4]

The originality of Greene's fable lies in its portrait of the ant. Aesop's
exemplar of prudence and foresight is introduced with a blackened
character.

The greedy miser thirsteth still for gaine,
His thrift is theft, his weale works others woe ...

Is Aesop's ant a greedy miser, whose thrift is *theft*? Is it said to *work others woe*? These surprising charges pick up the very accusations levelled against 'Shake-scene'. *Theft* reverts to 'an vpstart Crow, *beautified with our feathers*', and the idea that the ant injures others by its industry resembles 'an absolute *Iohannes fac totum*', the 'onely Shake-scene in a countrey' (i.e. one who puts other playwrights out of business). Again, the ant's nature is powerfully suggested in the phrase 'waspish little worme', and in its own words, 'Vse no intreats, I will relentlesse rest': like Shake-scene, it has a tiger's heart.

Elsewhere in *GWW* Greene also preferred not to accuse others too directly. He did not name the three dramatists or Shakespeare in his letter to his 'Quondam acquaintance', but left it to the reader to guess them. Since the fable of the ant and the grasshopper continues his previous complaints it places them in a new context that is more insidiously damaging. Whereas the overstatement in the Shake-scene passage is almost hysterical, and consequently self-defeating, the case against the ant seems more plausible, presented as it is from three points of view: the narrator first repudiates the grasshopper as a 'wanton', a speaker not to be trusted; the ant then partly accepts the grasshopper's view of itself, as thrifty and proud of it; the narrator endorses the more prejudicial view ('waspish little worme'); the ant endorses it too ('I will relentlesse rest'). Yet, as the grasshopper finally agrees that ants know best, the reader is prompted to feel that justice has been done, whereas the prudent ant, of course, has been painted in most unpleasant colours.

If we accept that Greene's ant glances back at Shakespeare, because the fable repeats three earlier charges against 'Shake-scene' (theft, injury to others, a tiger's heart), what else do we learn from Greene's thinly disguised invective? First, that he thought of Shakespeare as an 'olde acquaintance', and, fallen on evil days, had appealed to him for help. Second, the implications of 'the onely Shake-scene in a countrey' are clarified. Greene appears to have meant not merely 'the only supplier of plays' but one who 'in his owne conceit' was the central figure in the theatrical world. The ant is probably spokesman for 'those Puppets', those 'Anticks' who had rejected Greene (and this may explain why Greene's mind jumped from being 'forsaken' to the 'Tygers hart'). Third, the fable's insistence on the ant's thrift is revealing. In Caxton and other versions of Aesop the ant's thrift was implied; Greene repeats the word so often, as also others that develop the same thought (carefully prying, greedy miser, thriftie husband, labour, toile, toyling labour) that he manages to make thrift seem thoroughly inhuman – indeed, repulsive. The intended suggestion, I take it, is the same as that found in the second sentence after 'the onely Shake-scene in a countrey'. ('I knowe the best husband of you all will neuer proue an Vsurer, and the kindest of them all will neuer proue a kind nurse', meaning 'I know the best of *them* will prove an usurer').

*   *   *

At this point I must interrupt briefly in order to glance at Shakespeare's sonnets. At least three of the sonnets (110–12) are concerned with a 'vulgar scandal' that was deeply wounding. It arose from Shakespeare's professional activities, and he justified himself by saying that in a public situation one must adopt 'public manners'.

> O, for my sake do you with Fortune chide,
> The guilty goddess of my harmful deeds,
> That did not better for my life provide
> Than public means which public manners breeds.
> Thence comes it that my name receives a brand . . .

Some think that this refers to the disgrace of being an actor[5]. While actors were legally 'rogues and vagabonds', we have no reason to believe that Shakespeare's name was branded in the ordinary way of business. But we do know of one – and only one – public branding of his *name*, and I have argued that Greene's was a more wide-ranging and a more venomously personal attack than has been recognised. Could the sonnets refer to Greene? This is not an entirely new suggestion, for Shakespeare appears to go out of his way to drag in the name[6]:

> Your love and pity doth th'impression fill
> Which vulgar scandal stamp'd upon my brow;
> For what care I who calls me well or ill
> So you o'ergreen my bad, my good allow?

This is the first recorded use of *o'ergreen.* Why did Shakespeare coin the word?[7] It has been paraphrased as 'to cover with green . . . hence *fig.*, to cover so as to conceal a defect, embellish' (*OED*) – curious word, most easily explained as a punning allusion to *GWW* and its repercussions. (Apologising for not moderating the heat of Greene's anger in *GWW*, Henry Chettle acknowledged later in 1592 that 'diuers of worship' had reported Shakespeare's 'vprightnes of dealing', that is, had defended his good name – which is what 'o'ergreen my bad [name]' also suggests. Was the young man addressed in the sonnets one of the 'diuers of worship'?)

The dating of the sonnets remains disputed. Some place them at the turn of the century, or later. I am not convinced that all the sonnets were written at the same time, over a period of only three years or so; and if the early plays have been postdated, as I suggest below (pp. 54, 77), the sonnets could be moved back as well. Leaving these larger questions aside, however, it is surely quixotic *not* to connect sonnets 110 –12 and the one vulgar scandal that so neatly elucidates what they say.

*   *   *

Greene's 'Tygers hart', together with 'greedy miser' and 'Vsurer', conjures up a picture that is already familiar to students of Elizabethan drama – that of Philip Henslowe, the theatrical entrepreneur who helped out as banker for various groups of actors from 1592 and also carried on a lucrative business as pawn-broker or, as contemporaries will have said, as usurer. Whether or not theatre historians have been unfair to Henslowe, who could be generous to actors, pathetic appeals to him for financial assistance let us glimpse the humiliating poverty experienced by many a writer at this time.

> My Hinchlow I acquaynted you wth my necessity which I know you did in part supply but if you doe not help me to tenn shillings by this bearer by the living god I am vtterly disgract one ffryday night I will bring you papers to the valew of three acts Sr my occation is not ordynary that thus sodeynly I write . . .[8]

Greene's appeal to 'those Puppets' was also for money, for he was 'lying in extreame pouerty . . . comfortlesly languishing, hauing but one groat left'; and the 'waspish little worme' turned him away[9]. What I would tentatively suggest, therefore, is that in the period 1590–94, when the London acting companies were re-grouping and a new financial strategy was called for, not only Henslowe but others may have emerged as theatrical bankers or paymasters, one for each company; one other, as the far-sighted reader has guessed, being William Shakespeare.

Be that as it may, Greene certainly depicted the ant as well-to-do. While others starve it is 'fed with cates' (choice foods, delicacies). How then does this picture of a thrifty and thriving ant square with other accounts of Shakespeare? It is corroborated by several later witnesses, notably the records of his extraordinary financial success. He was the only actor of the period, except for Edward Alleyn, who made a fortune for himself; in addition, his talent for bargaining is referred to three times by his 'Loveinge good ffrend' Richard Quiney, and by others who clearly knew him well, in the Quiney correspondence of 1598.

(i) This is one speciall remembrance from vr fathers motion. It semeth bj him that our countriman, Mr Shaksper, is willinge to disburse some monei vpon some od yardeland or other att Shottri or neare about vs; he thinketh it a verj fitt patterne to move him to deale in the matter of our tithes. Bj the instruccions v can geve him theareof, and bj the frendes he can make therefore, we thinke it a faire marke for him to shoote att, and not unpossible to hitt. It obtained would advance him in deede, and would do vs muche good. Hoc movere, et quantum in te est permouere, ne necligas, hoc enim et sibi et nobis maximi erit momenti. Hic labor, hoc opus esset eximiae et gloriae et laudis sibi . . . (A. Sturley to R. Quiney, 24 January 1598)

(ii) Loveinge Contreyman, I am bolde of yowe as of a ffrende, craveinge yowre helpe with xxx^{li} vppon Mr Bushells & my securytee or Mr Myttons with me . . . Yowe shall ffrende me muche in helpeinge me out of all the debettes I owe in London, I thancke god, & muche quiet my mynde which wolde nott be indebeted. I am nowe towardes the Cowrte in hope of answer for the dispatche of my Buysenes. Yowe shall neither loase creddytt nor monney by me, the Lorde wyllinge . . . & yf we Bargaine farther yowe shalbe the paiemaster yowre self . . . (R. Quiney to W. Shakespeare, 25 October 1598)

(iii) Yow shalle, God wylling, receve from your wyfe by ye baylye, thys brynger, aswrance of x^s . . . . Yff yow bargen with Mr Sha . . or receve money therfor, brynge your money home yf yow maye, I see how knite stockynges be sold, ther ys gret byinge of them at Evysshome. (A. Quiney to R. Quiney, *c*. 30 October 1598)

(iv) Vr letter of the 25 of October came to mj handes the laste of the same att night per Grenwaj, which imported ... that our countriman Mr Wm. Shak. would procure vs monej, which I will like of as I shall heare when, and wheare, and howe; and I praj let not go that occasion if it may sort to any indifferent condicions ... (A. Sturley to R. Quiney, 4 November 1598)

Abraham Sturley was bailiff of Stratford in 1596, the year in which the dramatist's father, a former bailiff, sued for a grant of arms; and the tone of Richard Quiney's letter to Shakespeare is that of a friend, possibly a close friend, who assumes that his loving countryman will help him if he can. (Richard Quiney was Adrian's son; Richard's son Thomas was later to marry Shakespeare's daughter Judith). These men, no doubt in touch with all the latest gossip in Stratford, where Shakespeare had purchased New Place in 1597, did not expect financial negotiations with him to be easily settled. (i) One had to 'move him to deale'; and not only *movere* but *permovere*[10]. (ii) Shakespeare might gib at the 'securytee', and might want to 'Bargaine farther'. (iii) To 'bargen with Mr Sha.' would not be unusual. (iv) Most revealing of all is Sturley's refusal to jump for joy on hearing that Shakespeare would procure money – until he knows the conditions ('when, and wheare, and howe'). I deduce that hard conditions would not have surprised Sturley.

The Quiney correspondence supports Greene's picture of the thriving and thrifty ant. A loan of £30 would have been a very substantial sum, the equivalent of a five-figure sum in the devalued currency of 1981. Shakespeare was thought capable of raising it[11], and was expected to bargain shrewdly. The fact that Shakespeare took others to court, to retrieve smallish debts, points in the same direction[12] – that he was a hard-headed businessman, perhaps a money-lender as well. So, I think, does a less familiar allusion to 'thrifty' Shakespeare, which needs to be examined in greater detail. It occurs in *Ratseis Ghost* (1605), an account of the 'madde Prankes and Robberies' of the famous highwayman, Gamaliel Ratsey, who was executed on 26 March, 1605. The anonymous author tells how Ratsey met with a troop of players at an inn and asked them to entertain him with music ('let me heare your musicke, for I haue often gone to plaies more for musicke sake, then for action'). A week later he met the same players at another inn, and 'was desirous they should play a priuate play before him, which they did'. He paid them forty shillings, a generous fee, only to waylay them the next day and demand the return of the forty shillings with interest.

[And for you (sirra saies hee to the chiefest of them) thou hast a good

presence vpon a stage, me thinks thou darkenst thy merite by playing
in the country:] Get thee to London, for if one man were dead, they
will haue much neede of such a one as thou art. There would be none
in my opinion, fitter then thy selfe to play his parts: my conceipt is
such of thee, that I durst venture all the mony in my purse on thy
head, to play Hamlet with him for a wager. There thou shalt learne to
be frugall (for Players were neuer so thriftie as they are now about
London) & to feed vpon all men, to let none feede vpon thee; to make
thy hand a stranger to thy pocket, thy hart slow to performe thy
tongues promise: and when thou feelest thy purse well lined, buy thee
some place or Lordship in the Country, that growing weary of
playing, thy mony may there bring thee to dignitie and reputation:
[then thou needest care for no man, nor (*sic*) not for them that before
made thee prowd, with speaking their words vpon the Stage]. Sir, I
thanke you (quoth the Player) for this good counsell, I promise you I
will make vse of it; for I haue heard indeede, of some that haue gone to
London very meanly, and haue come in time to be exceeding wealthy.
[And in this presage and propheticall humor of mine, (sayes Ratsey)
kneele downe, Rise vp Sir Simon two shares and a halfe: Thou art now
one of my Knights, and the first Knight that euer was Player in
England.][13]

The passages that I have put in square brackets were omitted by
Chambers, who commented only that 'The weary player is more likely to
be Alleyn than Shakespeare'.[14] It should be said at once that the weary
player must be either Alleyn or Shakespeare, since no other actor had
acquired a fortune by 1605. But is he more likely to be Alleyn? Notice
that the author gibes twice at thrifty players who have become rich:
weary of acting, they can buy some place or lordship in the country; and
'some haue gone to London very meanly' and yet came to be 'exceeding
wealthy'. Now it happens that Alleyn was a Londoner born[15], so why
should he 'go to London'? The phrase fits Shakespeare, not Alleyn. And,
though Alleyn is remembered as the player who could afford to buy the
manor of Dulwich, it was not until 25 October 1605 that he 'took the
first step in the purchase of the manor of Dulwich, which was completed
by 1614'[16], whereas *Ratseis Ghost* was entered in the Stationers' Register
on 31 May 1605. True, Alleyn had bought leaseholds before 1605[17];
Shakespeare, however, had bought New Place in 1597, and his father had
applied for the grant of arms in 1596, so 'some *place* or *Lordship*' would be
a peculiarly appropriate thrust. It is significant, too, that Shakespeare
drops out of the actor-lists after *Sejanus* (1603)[18], which fits in with the

hint that the rich actor had grown 'weary of playing' by 1605. (Alleyn had stopped acting by this time as well.) Why, next, the sneer at hard-to-please dramatists ('then thou needest care for no man . . .')? Most of the dramatists were financially dependent on the players, and in no position to dictate to them; Shakespeare, however, being a 'sharer' could make actors 'care' for him, and we know that he 'instructed' them in their art[19]. Finally, 'Sir Simon two shares and a halfe' continues the attack on rich players. Who is intended? Alleyn's name was omitted from the patent issued to his colleagues in 1603[20], and it is assumed that he ceased to be a sharer at this time. Sir Simon ('Skinflint') harks back to frugal players, and either Burbage or Shakespeare might be the target, or indeed other King's Men who were sharers in their company and also in the Globe theatre. But Shakespeare, with his coat of arms and purchases of land, is the obvious share-pluralist one would think of in 1605 with pretensions to be 'the first Knight that euer was Player in England'.

'If one man were dead' must refer to Burbage, since Burbage was the celebrated Hamlet of his day. The passage therefore moves from Burbage and Hamlet to thrifty London players (which suggests the King's Men in the first instance), then to one very rich and frugal player, then to dramatists who make actors 'care' for them, then to 'some that have gone to London very meanly' and acquired wealth there, then to Sir Simon two shares and a half. Every one of these later gibes points at Shakespeare, some quite explicitly, whereas only one fits Alleyn (weary of playing, he had begun to invest in property). Although the passage slithers cleverly between singulars and plurals, all the accusations converge on one man: the context therefore drives us to take the 'weary player' with disgustingly thrifty habits to be Shakespeare, whether or not we think of Alleyn as well.

This, then, is a second personal attack very like the fable of the ant and the grasshopper. As in the case of *GWW*, which was far from disinterested, we must of course beware of taking it literally or too seriously. The author of *Ratseis Ghost* goes on to describe, with relish, how the highwayman robbed the rich (a tapster, a grazier, a lawyer) and gave to the poor: like Ratsey himself, the pamphleteer might have said 'I spare not them that are rich' (E3a). Wealth is wickedness, so the rich player was bound to be represented as a villain.

In a survey of the evidence for an 'ungentle' Shakespeare, we must also look at his record as a businessman. Not all the surviving documents are informative, but several lend themselves to more than the one prevailing interpretation. For example, William Wayte in 1596 craved sureties of the peace 'versus Willelmum Shakspere Franciscum Langley Dorotheam

Soer uxorem Johannis Soer & Annam Lee ob metum mortis &'.[21]
Nothing more is known about Dorothy Soer or Anne Lee; Francis
Langley, though, happened to be the owner of the Swan Theatre where,
it has been conjectured, Shakespeare's company performed in 1596. Was
Shakespeare's name bracketed with Langley's, as has been suggested,
because Langley's enemies wished to vex the players until they vacated
the Swan, thus 'depriving Langley of income'[22]? A curiously round-about
way of expelling a large company of actors, to crave sureties of the peace
against one! Let us remember that Langley had more in common with
Shakespeare than a financial interest in the theatre, if the 1596 suit refers
to the dramatist, as is generally believed. Langley was a money-lender,
and was described by a victim as 'of a covetous and greedy mind' – the
traditional anti-usury rhetoric, employed by Greene's grasshopper against
the ant, but in Langley's case fully deserved; a fascinating recent biography presents him as an unprincipled adventurer, a very unpleasant
customer indeed[23]. Shakespeare's money-lending could have begun as
early as 1592[24]; we hear of it again in the Sturley-Quiney letters of 1598,
and in 1604 and 1608, when he sued Philip Rogers and John Adden-
brooke for small debts[25] – so his being associated with the unscrupulous
Langley in 1596 raises questions, whatever other common interests they
may have had.

A second usurer played a more visible part in Shakespeare's life. John
Combe, reputedly the wealthiest man in Stratford, had become rich by
charging borrowers the legal rate of ten per cent; in the first published
Life of Shakespeare (1709), Nicholas Rowe told

> a Story almost still remember'd in that Country, that he [Shakespeare]
> had a particular Intimacy with Mr. *Combe*, an old Gentleman noted
> thereabouts for his Wealth and Usury: It happen'd, that in a pleasant
> Conversation amongst their common Friends, Mr. *Combe* told *Shake-*
> *spear* in a laughing manner, that he fancy'd, he intended to write his
> Epitaph, if he happen'd to out-live him; and since he could not know
> what might be said of him when he was dead, he desir'd it might be
> done immediately: Upon which *Shakespear* gave him these four Verses.

> *Ten in the Hundred lies here ingrav'd,*
> *'Tis a Hundred to Ten, his Soul is not sav'd.*
> *If any Man ask, Who lies in this Tomb?*
> *Oh! ho! quoth the Devil, 'tis my* John-a-Combe.

But the Sharpness of the Satyr is said to have stung the Man so
severely, that he never forgave it.

Biographers have not taken this pretty story too seriously, since similar epitaphs were ascribed to John Hoskins (1566–1638), and one version reached print by 1608 ('Ten in the hundred lies under this stone, / And a hundred to ten to the devil he's gone'.)

> If there is anything in the story [wrote Chambers], Shakespeare can at most . . . have adapted verses which he knew from Hoskins or another. Rowe's notion of Combe's resentment is negatived by the legacy [to Shakespeare] in Combe's will.[26]

What is more significant than Rowe's final sentence is that several seventeenth-century visitors to Stratford heard the story of the epitaph, the earliest one in 1634, and that Rowe could not have known either Combe's will or Shakespeare's. (Combe left Shakespeare £5 in 1613, and Shakespeare in 1616 left 'to mr Thomas Combe my Sword'; Thomas was John Combe's nephew and heir.) The two wills confirm that the two families were friendly. Whether or not Shakespeare 'gave' Combe the four verses, there is no reason to doubt his 'particular Intimacy' with a noted usurer.

A word now about a business venture dating from 1598 – Shakespeare's store of ten quarters of malt, a commodity in which well-to-do Stratfordians invested 'somewhat to the impoverishment of their neighbours in a time of dearth'[27]. A Council letter of 1597 described hoarders more emphatically as 'wycked people in condicions more lyke to wolves or cormerants than to naturall men'[28]. Though not a personal criticism of one man, this again helps to place Shakespeare for us. His business interests and associates have a smack of Shylock about them; he that toucheth malt shall be defiled.

No single document gives a more revealing glimpse of Shakespeare the businessman than his own will, which he altered a month before he died, on 25 March 1616. That his alterations indicate a lack of confidence in his new son-in-law, Thomas Quiney (who had married Judith on 10 February 1616), was long suspected. It is now known that he had good reason to mistrust Quiney, who was forced to appear in open court in Stratford parish church on 26 March 1616 and confess 'that he had had carnal copulation with Margaret Wheeler'[29]. Margaret and her child had died a few days earlier, and were buried on 15 March. Whether or not this was 'the biggest scandal that Stratford had seen for years', it was bound to be talked about when two such prominent families were concerned. So Shakespeare, whose signatures were already shaky when his will was first drawn up, probably in January 1616, sent for his solicitor and had his will re-drafted to protect Judith – his feelings, we may suppose, as cordial as Mr. Bennet's for Mr. Wickham. Judith, he now decreed, is to receive an additional sum of £150 if still alive three years after her father's death; if she dies within the three years, the money is to go to Shakespeare's grand-daughter and sister (i.e. not to Quiney); if she lives for three years, the money is to be invested by his executors and 'not to be paied vnto her soe long as she shalbe marryed' (i.e. not to Quiney), unless 'such husbond as she shall att thend of the saied three Yeares be marryed vnto or attaine after doe sufficientlie Assure vnto her & thissue of her bodie landes Awnswereable to the porcion by this my will gyven vnto her'. The implications are obvious, and unpleasant. Quiney is not to be trusted with his wife's money; the marriage may not last; Quiney is not the man to provide an 'answerable portion'. Can we imagine that fellow-Stratfordians, when the news leaked out, spoke of a 'gentle will'? Almost certainly Shakespeare's last word as a businessman, it reminds me of qualities that we have noticed several times: hard-headed realism where money is concerned, and a willingness to take tough action that will anger others. The treatment of Quiney, though no doubt justified, helps us to understand what the Robert Greenes of the world chose to call the 'tiger's heart' and the relentlessness of a waspish nature.

(II) 'GENTLE' SHAKESPEARE

Less needs to be said about an entirely different view of Shakespeare, one that presents him as seen by his admirers. A. C. Bradley brought much of the evidence together in 'Shakespeare the Man'[30] – still the most perceptive of all such studies – and, since I partly disagree with him, I begin with his essay.

Bradley was particularly impressed by one 'eye-witness to Shakespeare the Man', Ben Jonson, who coined a notable phrase. 'I lov'd the man, and doe honour his memory (on this side Idolatry) as much as any. Hee was (indeed) honest, and of an open, and free nature'. These last words could also apply to many of the tragic heroes, Bradley observed. The sufferings of 'free and open natures are Shakespeare's favourite tragic subject'[31]; and the poet of the sonnets belongs to the same species, a free and open nature vulnerable to those he loves, betrayed by the Friend and the Dark Lady.

So far so good. But when one tries to imagine the day-to-day behaviour of a free and open nature, there are difficulties. 'Readers of Shakespeare, I believe, imagine him to have been not only sweet-tempered but modest and unassuming'[32]. Bradley here subscribes to the 'sweet Shakespeare' myth, which grew out of early allusions to the poet's mellifluous style and had little to do with Shakespeare the man. A marginal note in W. Covell's *Polimanteia* (1595), in a passage praising the 'sweete, and well arte-tuned strings' of English poets, is the first recorded example. Neither Ariosto nor Tasso, writes Covell, is 'worthie to make compare with your truelie eternizing *Elizas* stile'; he commends 'diuine *Spenser*', Daniel's 'sweete refined muse' and lists various poems, adding in the margin '*All praise / worthy. / Lucrecia/Sweet Shak- / speare. / Eloquent / Gaueston. / Wanton / Adonis.*' The context puts it beyond doubt that Covell refers to nothing more than a style of writing; and the second and third allusions to 'sweet Shakespeare' continue in the same tradition.

the sweete wittie soule of *Ouid* liues in mellifluous & hony-tongued *Shakespeare,* witnes his *Venus* and *Adonis,* his *Lucrece,* his sugred Sonnets among his priuate friends, &c. (Francis Meres, 1598)

And *Shakespeare* thou, whose hony-flowing Vaine,
(Pleasing the World) thy Praises doth obtaine.
Whose *Venus,* and whose *Lucrece* (sweete, and chaste)
Thy Name in fames immortall Booke haue plac't. (R. Barnfield, 1598)[33]

Such allusions to a writer's style tell us no more about his personality than in the case of Sir Nicholas Bacon of whose 'sweete and sugred eloquence' we hear in 1585[34]. It was a hackneyed formula, used of many others, and we meet it again in the Cambridge *Parnassus* play of c. 1599, where a simpleton, Gullio, misquotes from *Venus and Adonis* and Ingenioso exclaims sarcastically 'Sweete Mr. Shakespeare!'; later Gullio recites in Shakespeare's 'vein' ('O sweet Mr. Shakespeare!') and is ecstatic when Ingenioso does the same ('I'le worshipp sweet Mr. Shakespeare').

All the allusions to 'sweet' Shakespeare recorded in his life-time refer back to his 'vein', or poetic style. Only after his death was Shakespeare the man described as 'sweet' – 'Sweet Swan of *Auon*!' (Jonson) – but so were many others after their deaths, for the word is one of the conventions of elegy. Spenser, shortly after he died, was called 'A sweeter swan then euer song in Poe'[35]. In Iohn Philip's *The Life and Death of Sir Phillip Sidney* (1587) we find 'This *Phenix* sweet *Sidney*' (sig. A2), and other elegies for *Astrophel* employed the word liberally. Unfortunately the myth of 'sweet Shakespeare' amalgamated with the myth of the Child of Nature ('sweetest Shakespeare, fancy's child'), and with yet another, the myth of 'easie numbers' ('Warble his native wood-notes wild'). In the upshot it was not surprising that Rowe's *Life* of 1709 adopted the myth and added a few fine flourishes.

> Besides the advantages of his Wit, he was in himself a good-natur'd Man, of great sweetness in his Manners, and a most agreeable Companion . . . His exceeding Candor and good Nature must certainly have inclin'd all the gentler Part of the World to love him . . .[36]

The myth of 'gentle Shakespeare' developed similarly. Although it has been said that 'the impressions of contemporaries sometimes find their distillation in a single apt epithet that clings to a name . . . Shakespeare is enshrined in consciousness as Gentle Will Shakespeare'[37], we must again beware of misreading the evidence. Bradley had written, in much the same spirit, after quoting Jonson's verses, 'This figure that thou seest here put, / It was for gentle Shakespeare cut' – 'so Jonson writes of the portrait in the Folio, and the same adjective ''gentle'' is used elsewhere of Shakespeare'. Where, exactly? It is a curious fact, apparently forgotten by those who are attracted to a 'gentle Shakespeare', that open, unequivocal tributes to his gentleness only appeared in print after his death[38], in the Folio, in two poems signed by Ben Jonson. The second contained the lines

> Yet must I not giue Nature all: Thy Art
> My gentle *Shakespeare,* must enioy a part.

How a man impressed others in his life-time is not necessarily indicated by memorial verses written some years after his death. Panegyric usually falls back on well-worn phrases; and, as recent studies have shown, the image of the poet in any age usually follows a dominant model[39]. In the late Elizabethan age Spenser and (for different reasons) Sidney were the dominant figures – gentle Colin Clout and gentle Astrophel[40] – so gentle Shakespeare again conforms to a stereotype. But what of '*my* gentle Shakespeare'? The possessive loses some of its force when we see it as Jonson's characteristic gesture – 'my Roe', 'my Wroth', 'my Burges' etc.[41] Add Jonson's tribute to Ferrabosco, 'my lou'd Alphonso', and to 'Master Arth: Squib' –

> What I am not, and what I faine would be,
> Whilst I informe my selfe, I would teach thee,
> My gentle *Arthur* . . .[42]

– and we begin to wonder whether the phrasing of 'My gentle Shakespeare' tells us more about the dead poet or the living one.

Jonson's very special relationship with Shakespeare is also relevant. The man who had said so often, and overbearingly, 'that Shakespeare wanted art'[43], was bound to recall, when offering what was in effect a public apology ('Yet must I not giue Nature all: Try Art, / My gentle *Shakespeare*, must enioy a part'), his rival's tolerance towards himself. And Jonson's special relationship with the world at large is also to the point. Accustomed to see himself as more learned, more 'artistic' and more worthy than anyone else, is it surprising that Jonson allowed a note of protectiveness, even of condescension, to intrude into one of his most generous poems? I sense that faintly jarring note in 'my gentle Shakespeare',[44] the stronger speaking of the weaker; it is unmistakable, of course, in 'though thou hadst small *Latine,* and lesse *Greeke*'.

Jonson, therefore, coined a phrase that tells us less than we would like about Shakespeare the man. He adopted the dominant image of the 'gentle' poet; he described Shakespeare from a very special viewpoint, that of a competitor who sees, probably for the first time, the unparalleled achievement of the other's 'works' and, for complicated personal reasons, feels a need to cheer himself up. Hence 'my gentle Shakespeare'. It should be noted, though, that Jonson also knew an ungentle Shakespeare. He believed that the dead man's 'minde, and manners' appear in his lines,

> In each of which, he seemes to shake a Lance,
> As brandish't at the eyes of Ignorance.

In his lines – and also in his name. And the vigour of 'shake-spear', the potential toughness, is again present in Jonson's final image:

> Shine forth, thou Starre of *Poets,* and with rage,
> Or influence, chide, or cheere the drooping Stage.

This refers to 1623. We are entitled to assume, however, that the poetic image expands upon the dead man's 'minde, and manners'. He chided and cheered his colleagues, as one might expect from the leading sharer of his company. He even chided angrily.

Two other early allusions appear to support the tradition of a sweet and gentle Shakespeare. We hear in passing of '*friendly SHAKE-SPEARE'S Tragedies*' (A. Scoloker, 1604), and of 'so deere lou'd a neighbor' (W. Barksted, 1607). Examine each passage in its context, though, and new questions arise. Scoloker's remarks come in the middle of a spoof epistle,

'To the mighty, learned, and ancient Potentate, QUISQUIS' etc. –

> *It* [viz. an epistle to the reader] *should be like the never-too-well-read*
> Arcadia, *where the Prose and Verse, Matter and Words, are like his*
> *Misstress's eyes! one still excelling another, and without corrival! or to come*
> *home to the vulgar's element, like friendly SHAKE-SPEARE'S Tragedies,*
> *where the Comedian rides, when the Tragedian stands on tiptoe. Faith, it*
> *should please all, like Prince* HAMLET! *But, in sadness, then it were to be*
> *feared, he* [the author] *would run mad. In sooth, I will not be moonsick, to*
> *please! nor out of my wits, though I displease all! What? Poet! are you in*
> *Passion, or out of Love? This is as strange as true!*
>
> *Well, well! If I seem mystical or tyrannicall; whether I be a fool or a*
> *Lord's-Ingle; all's one! . . . .* [45]

Since Scoloker writes tongue-in-cheek, one is driven to wonder whether,
initially, *Hamlet* failed to 'please all', which may have been what Gabriel
Harvey meant when he wrote, at about this time, that 'The younger sort
takes much delight in Shakespeares Venus, & Adonis: but his Lucrece, &
his tragedie of Hamlet, Prince of Denmarke, haue it in them, to please the
wiser sort'[46]. That the tragedies should be thought 'the vulgar's element'
also seems strange (only *Julius Caesar, Hamlet* and *Othello* would have been
written by 1604). Irony once suspected, we recall that a reliable source
described Shakespeare as the opposite of 'friendly', one who, if invited,
sent his excuses[47]. I do not wish to press the point, but only to note that
Scoloker's drift is 'mystical', as he says, and open to more than one
interpretation.

Barksted's compliment can also be read in two ways. In occurs in the
final stanza of *Mirrha The Mother of Adonis,* a narrative poem, clearly
influenced by *Venus and Adonis,* which deals with the events that supposedly preceded Shakespeare's story. Mirrha refuses Cupid's love; to
punish her, Cupid kindles 'an infernall and vnnam'd desire' – Mirrha
lusts for her father, conceives a child by him, is turned into a tree, and as a
tree brings forth a child, Adonis; the child grows up, and Venus loves
him. Barksted concludes by beginning the Venus and Adonis story, then
breaks off –

> But stay my Muse in thine owne confines keepe,
> & wage not warre with so deere lou'd a neighbor
> But hauing sung thy day song, rest and sleepe
> preserve thy small fame & his greater fauor:

His Song was worthie merrit (*Shakspeare* hee)
sung the faire blossome, thou the withered tree
Laurell is due to him, his art and wit
hath purchast it, *Cypres* thy brow will fit.[48]

Biographers[49] who report no more than that Barksted called Shakespeare 'so deere lou'd a neighbor' may lead readers to imagine that the two writers lived next door, and that neighbour Shakespeare, sweet and gentle, inspired affection. But Barksted more probably refers to literary territory, not personal domicile: the poets' literary 'confines' adjoin, so they are literary neighbours. That Shakespeare the man was 'so deere lou'd' remains possible; the context suggests, however, that Barksted was thinking of the popularity of *Venus and Adonis,* a poem that had run through nine or ten editions by 1607, whose author was 'deere lou'd' by the general public.

So much for allusions, the external evidence; in addition we have to examine the internal evidence, the plays and poems. The tradition of a sweet and gentle Shakespeare proved so irresistible, I believe, not only because allusions were not scrutinised carefully but because his own writings have exerted a semi-concealed yet powerful influence. For example, both *sweet* and *gentle* are favourite epithets for some of the poet's favourite characters, and are used by these characters in turn for those they respect or love. Is it not natural to infer that they express qualities that Shakespeare valued highly, and that they reflect his personality? 'Kneel not, gentle Portia. – I should not need, if you were gentle Brutus.' 'His life was gentle.' ''Tis sweet and commendable in your nature, Hamlet.' 'Good night, sweet prince.' Look at such passages in context, however, and a different picture emerges. They occur when one character appeals to another, or pacifies, or commends the dead: conscious or sub-conscious tactics are involved, cajolery ('I *know* you to be sweet-natured, although you try to hide it'), making amends to the defeated, etc. Such conjuring-tricks are most evident in the sonnets, especially when they are simultaneously formal and intimate. 'Thy self thy foe, to thy sweet self too cruel' (1. 8); 'Thou of thyself thy sweet self dost deceive' (4. 10). The poet makes all he can of one side of the Friend and, one feels, almost coaxes it into being. In the plays' death-speeches convention dictated, again – as it still does – that one dwelt on the best side of the dead.

The existence of something like an Homeric epithet for 'sweet Hamlet' or 'gentle Brutus' by no means guarantees that that is the full story. It refers to one side of a complex character, sometimes (as in the case of

Hamlet) not the side that is most visible. We may believe it to be wishful thinking, or the far side of the moon. Can we discount Hamlet's enacted ferocity, or Brutus' blood-smearing ritual, 'up to the elbows'? Where Shakespeare himself is concerned we should surely allow for a similar complexity.

A word now about the sonnets. Although literary exercises in their strenuous cultivation of one or more well-born friends, and their use of the conventions of courtly poetry, the sonnets tell so unusual a story that it is widely believed to be based on personal experience. If we accept this view, as I think we must, the poet's mild expostulations when his 'friend' steals his lady could be deemed sweet and gentle –

> Take all my loves, my love, yea take them all . . .
> I do forgive thy robb'ry, gentle thief . . .
> That thou hast her, it is not all my grief,
> And yet it may be said I lov'd her dearly;
> That she hath thee is of my wailing chief,
> A loss in love that touches me more nearly.[50]

Before we condemn the poet's attitude as excessively gentle and forgiving – like Valentine, who surrenders Silvia to his friend in *The Two Gentlemen of Verona* – we must be clear about the individuals concerned. The poet writes of his 'love' of the lady, yet leaves no doubt that she is a sexual freebooter, probably a high-class courtesan; having succumbed to her charms, he knows that he cannot trust her vows, that she humiliates him, that their relationship is founded on deceit (No. 138, etc.). Napoleon, we are told, when infatuated by such a lady, had to 'take his turn', and was kept waiting while she attended to another friend; he did not like it and, according to one source, recognising his rival as the Duc d'Enghien, later had him seized, tried, and executed. How vindictive and ungentlemanly! Shakespeare's attitude differed significantly from Valentine's, because the Dark Lady was no Silvia, and from Napoleon's, because Shakespeare saw that to quarrel about 'the bay where all men ride', a woman who was 'the wide world's common place' (No. 137), would be ridiculous. He made the best of a bad job, knowing that his friend was not the seducer but the seduced (No. 41).

In the triangle situation of the sonnets the poet's behaviour may be described as *civilised* – and that, after all, is what *gentle* could mean in his day. He did not rage at his friend for betraying him; on another occasion, when a rival poet tried to get the better of him, he appeared 'tongue-tied' because he refused to fight back (cf. p. 106, below). The civilised man sometimes seems soft, and the sonnets confirm that in certain situations Shakespeare might give such an impression – refusing to stoop to the level of those around him. There are other indications that he was not easily drawn into a quarrel; he opposed Jonson in the War of the Theatres, and Jonson recognised that he was drawn in unwillingly.

> Onely amongst them, I am sorry for
> Some better natures, by the rest so drawne,
> To run in that vile line.[51]

So, too, there were Jonson's repeated snipings at his rival's art, which only drew a riposte after many years[52].

Since *gentle* could mean something like *civilised,* it is interesting that Chettle wrote in 1592 that he had seen Shakespeare's 'demeanor no lesse ciuill than he exelent in the qualitie he professes.' For Chettle's *ciuill* probably meant civilised, well-bred (*OED* 8, 9); and perhaps Jonson's phrase, 'gentle Shakespeare', was half-intended to point in the same direction. Other contemporary allusions bear out that Shakespeare struck those who knew him as well-bred, notably two by John Davies of Hereford, (i) from *Microcosmos* (1603), (ii) from *The Scourge of Folly* (1610).

> (i) And though the *stage* doth staine pure gentle *bloud,*
>   Yet generous yee are in *minde* and *moode.*

> (ii) Some say (good *Will*) which I, in sport, do sing,
>   Had'st thou not plaid some Kingly parts in sport,
>   Thou hadst bin a companion for a *King*;
>   And, beene a King among the meaner sort.
>   Some others raile; but, raile as they thinke fit,
>   Thou hast no rayling, but, a raigning Wit.[53]

Here, again, it is suggested that Shakespeare was disinclined to be a quarreller. Davies, like Chettle, thought Shakespeare's demeanour easy, gentlemanly, unaggressive – and such a man might well have appeared to Jonson, the most talented quarreller of his age, almost too sweet and gentle for his own good.

(III) SYNTHESIS

While the myth of a sweet and gentle Shakespeare must be challenged, let us be clear where we stand. Heminge and Condell published the Folio 'onely to keepe the memory of so worthy a Friend, & Fellow aliue as was our Shakespeare'; Jonson wrote his verses 'To the memory of my beloved, The Author, Mr. William Shakespeare', and said in prose 'I lov'd the man.' Good witnesses, who certify that Shakespeare could inspire love and friendship. But so could Jonson, and we do not hear of him as gentle Ben. Perhaps Scoloker really thought Shakespeare 'friendly', and Barksted lived next-door and loved him dearly; if, though, we interpret the last two differently, no one, before 1623, referred to Shakespeare the man as sweet and gentle (as distinct from gentle = gentlemanly), except, perhaps, for Richard Quiney, who wanted to borrow £30. (Quiney addressed him in 1598 as his 'Loveinge good ffrend & contreymann Mr Wm. Shackespere'). The external evidence for a sweet and gentle poet derives from Jonson's two posthumous tributes, and very little else; and, as I have suggested, Jonson's account of his dead friend was influenced by literary conventions, by his own unusual personality, and by a special love-hate relationship with 'my beloved'.

What of the external evidence pointing in the opposite direction? Some of it has long been available. Though we may prefer to disregard Greene's rancour in *GWW*, depicting a 'tiger's heart' and relentlessness towards an old acquaintance, there are other signs of something similar. When Greene hit about him so recklessly in his death-bed confessions, two dramatists were displeased. 'With neither of them that take offence was I acquainted,' said Chettle, but Shakespeare, and 'diuers of worship' who were his friends, made themselves known immediately, and extracted a public apology. When Jaggard reissued *The Passionate Pilgrim* in 1612, Heywood reported that Shakespeare was 'much offended with M. *Iaggard* that (altogether unknowne to him) presumed to make so bold with his name'; one of the two surviving copies of the 1612 edition contains a cancel title-page, from which Shakespeare's name has been removed – again, immediate action, immediate results[54]. Other bits of evidence are equally significant. The publication of 'bad' quartos was thought to bring 'iniury and disgrace' to their authors: the issuing of three Shakespearian 'good' quartos to replace the bad must have been initiated by the dramatist[55] – an unusual step, doubtlessly taken because he resented the injury to his reputation, and probably opposed by his own colleagues and by the stationers. Once more, effective action. Best of all, we have Shakespeare's will, and we now understand why it had to be altered. A sweet and gentle Shakespeare is, in part, the fabrication of bardolatry; a very different man, sharp and business-like, speaks to us from some of the principal life-records.

How may we reconcile these different impressions? Ben Jonson provides an instructive parallel. We know from Drummond that 'of all stiles he loved most to be named honest, and hath of that ane hundreth letters so naming him'[56]. And yet, can we really describe as honest (Lat. *honestus,* honourable) the man who told Drummond 'he thought the use of a maide, nothing jn comparison to ye wantoness of a wyfe & would never haue ane other Mistress', and that when he was 'once so taken the Good man said, I would not believe yee would abuse my house so'[57]? True, he was not sober. But *in vino veritas*; and the scurrilousness of Jonson's epigrams, as also his delight in every kind of roguery, in the plays and in his conversations, indicates that honest Ben was only half of the man.

As with Jonson, so with Shakespeare. 'Gentle' Shakespeare was only half the man, and a memorable phrase grossly oversimplifies the evidence that survives; or, more correctly, it gives us just one side of a man no less myriad-minded than many-sided. For, having stumbled through the mists of sentimentality and tradition, we discover that the sign-posts always point two ways at once. Some thought him a hoarding miser, others 'open, and free'. There can be no doubt that he lent money on 'condicions', and that he encouraged theatre-goers to rejoice in the fall of usurers (*Merchant of Venice, Timon*). He wrote a play to prove that 'virtue is the true nobility' (*All's Well*), having probably himself financed his father's application for a grant of arms, and he harshly satirised the ambition to be 'spacious in the possession of dirt' (*Hamlet*, V. 2. 88) and a year or two later paid £320 for arable land in Old Stratford. He was attacked as an upstart crow, and admired as one fit to have 'bin a companion for a *King*'[58]. He went out of his way to have the Duke in *Twelfth Night* say 'Let still the woman take / An elder than herself' (II. 4. 28), and was himself marrried to a wife eight years his senior.

Let us turn briefly to another contradiction – seventeenth century gossip about Shakespeare's drinking-exploits, together with Aubrey's testimony that 'he was not a company keeper lived in Shoreditch, wouldnt be debauched, & if invited to writ; he was in paine'. Aubrey's source was William Beeston, the son of Christopher Beeston, Shakespeare's fellow in the Lord Chamberlain's company, whereas the first 'drinking' story comes from John Ward, vicar of Stratford (1662–81), who also swallowed the incredible rumour that the dramatist 'spent att ye Rate of a 1,000 *l.* a year, as I have heard'. Nevertheless, other early anecdotes give some support to a convivial Shakespeare – for example, Fuller's about 'the *wit-combates* betwixt him and *Ben Johnson*'[59], whether or not we locate them in the Mermaid Tavern. Here, I see no real difficulty. The dramatist might have been happy to drink with friends while refusing invitations from strangers; or, like Milton, another industrious writer, he could have permitted himself a gaudy day every so often.

Indeed, none of the contradictions that I have mentioned presents a real difficulty on its own: what is surprising is that there are so many. Biographers, faced with contradictions, are inclined to choose between them, and will happily settle for a gentle Shakespeare, loved by all, whose financial transactions were sweetness and light. At the risk of seeming a damnable both-sides rogue, I would suggest that where there are two views of Shakespeare they may both be right. A hostile witness should not be ignored simply because he is a hostile witness; gossip is often misguided, and often correct. The surviving evidence is complicated and gives us – as might have been expected – a complicated man.

Shakespeare the man, as I see him, differs from the older, sentimental model in being harder, when necessary, and more business-like. (Perhaps this revaluation was inevitable. The image of 'gentle Shakespeare' became fixed in the seventeenth and eighteenth centuries, whereas the full extent of his business interests only emerged in the nineteenth and twentieth centuries.) Gentle, friendly, open and free, certainly, among his friends – 'yet, notwithstanding, being incens'd, he is flint'. We first hear of him in London when an old acquaintance, in great trouble, appeals to him for help, and is refused – which provoked Greene's death-bed attack; and our final glimpse of him is as his own death approaches and he alters his will, thus adding to the humiliation of his son-in-law. In between 1592 and 1616 there came many plays and many business ventures, but the essential man remained the same. While we like to think of him as a Hamlet figure, he also appears to have been endowed with the ruthless efficiency of Henry v. He could 'imitate the action of the tiger'. Not for nothing did Greene select the line from *3 Henry vi;* he wanted to point accusingly at a 'Tygers hart': unfairly, maliciously, it may be – but, I believe, not entirely beside the mark.

2
The Writer

In this chapter I shall try to trace Shakespeare's impact as a writer. When did contemporaries begin to recognise his special excellence? What in particular did they admire? Was he really 'rated at something like his true value'? A great deal of contemporary evidence survives – and some of it, again, has been misinterpreted and needs to be reconsidered in its contemporary setting.

(I) EARLY RECOGNITION

First, let us examine Shakespeare's 'breakthrough' as a writer. Once more we have to begin with Greene's *Groats-Worth of Witte* (*GWW*), where the Aesopian allusion in 'an vpstart Crow, beautified with our feathers' has caused trouble. Was Greene thinking of a '*new* upstart writer', as Malone paraphrased it in the eighteenth century[1]? If so, that would be important; it would imply that Shakespeare arrived on the literary scene later than Greene and the three dramatists he was addressing (Marlowe, Nashe and Peele); for, since Marlowe and Nashe began their literary careers in 1587 and 1589, Greene thus seems to confirm the traditional date for Shakespeare's *début* in London, 1590. E. K. Chambers still took the 'vpstart Crow' to mean a 'new upstart writer' in 1930, but two other explanations have been proposed: the upstart might be either an actor turned dramatist, or a writer from an inferior background, one who cannot claim to be a scholar and a gentleman like Greene and his friends[2]. Refer to the historical context and we discover that such social upstarts were much discussed. Satirists had for some time jeered at social climbers when Greene's protégé, Nashe, joined the band-wagon in 1589, singling out uneducated writers who pretend to be scholars and 'in disguised array [vaunt] *Ouids* and *Plutarchs* plumes as theyr owne', or steal sentences from English translations of Seneca, who 'will affoord you whole Hamlets, I should say handfuls, of Tragicall speeches'. In the very

25

year of *GWW*, 1592, Nashe returned to the fray in *Pierce Penilesse*[3], and Greene himself joined in by writing *A Quip for an Upstart Courtier,* where the word *upstart* occurs frequently in the sense 'social climber' rather than specifically 'newcomer'. The upstart crow of 1592 therefore need not imply a new writer. A small point – but, as will be seen, not unimportant when we try to date Shakespeare's beginnings and 'breakthrough' as a dramatist[4].

Greene's other gibe at Shakespeare, that he thinks himself 'an absolute *Iohannes fac totum*', has attracted less attention. What did he wish to suggest? The *Oxford English Dictionary* tells us that the forms *Dominus factotum* and *Magister factotum* were in use before 1592, giving *GWW* as the first entry for *Johannes factotum.* Early examples of *Dominus factotum* ('one who controls everything') are not hard to find[5], but, apart from the French equivalent, recorded by *OED* (*Frère Jean Factotum,* 1590), I have not seen *Johannes factotum* before 1592. Greene therefore introduced a new term, or chose a very uncommon variant of a familiar term, to sneer once more at social status – a 'Jack of all trades'. Upstart crow and *Johannes factotum,* in short, both point the same way.

While Greene need not have thought of Shakespeare as a new writer, there are signs in *GWW* that he already saw him as an established writer. Greene assumed that the name Shakespeare was sufficiently well known for a punning allusion to 'Shake-scene' to be comprehensible, and even that a single line from one of the plays would be recognised. This is puzzling when we compare the evidence of the first quarto title-pages. How can we explain the fact that five or six years after *GWW* the publishers of the plays remained unaware or unpersuaded of the magic of Shakespeare's name, and omitted it from the title-pages? *Titus Andronicus* (1594), *The Contention* (1594), *The True Tragedy* (1595), *Richard III* (1597), *Romeo* (1597), *Richard II* (1597) and *1 Henry IV* (1598) all failed to state the writer's name, a 'breakthrough' that began in 1598. (*Richard III* (1598), *Richard II* (1598) and *Love's Labour's Lost* (1598) all blazoned the name.) It may well be that the publication of Francis Meres' *Palladis Tamia* (1598: SR entry 7 September), with, its enthusiastic praise of Shakespeare, and its list of twelve of his plays, proved decisive in establishing his name with the book-trade in general: the only play-text of 1598 without the name, *1 Henry IV,* was entered in the Stationers' Register before *Palladis Tamia* (on 25 February). Nevertheless *Locrine* (1595), with the misleading title-page assertion 'By W.S.', surely indicates that the only dramatist of note with these initials would be easily identified, and confirms the inference from *GWW* that Shakespeare's name was known before 1598[6]. A possible explanation of the carelessness of publishers who omitted it from their title-pages until 1597–8 is that the humble author failed to insert it in his manuscripts. The manuscripts are lost, of course, but the evidence from early quartos tallies with that afforded by entries in the Stationers' Register. (The first SR entry to indicate the authorship of a Shakespearian play is the double entry for *Much Ado* and *2 Henry IV* of 23 August 1600, concluding with the words 'Wrytten by master Shakespere' – words which, if copied from a play manuscript, he is unlikely to have written himself.)

A complicating factor is that we cannot tell how widely a dramatist's name would be known when a play was performed, before its publication. In *Histriomastix* the players arrive in a town and 'cry' a forthcoming performance, 'Come to the Towne-house and see a Play'; they are asked 'What's your playes name? Maisters whose men are ye?' (B4b, C1a), but no one asks the playwright's name. While the professional companies may have employed such 'Pagliacci' methods on provincial tours, one suspects that they had more sophisticated publicity in London, where some of the leading writers would be personally known. Later in *Histriomastix* it is said of the playwright Posthaste that it 'is as dangerous to read his name at the playe-dore / As a printed bill on a plague dore' (E4b), i.e. he doesn't attract customers. Bentley, apparently unaware of this interesting hint, cited a letter by Dryden (4 March 1699) – 'the printing an author's name in a play-bill is a new manner of proceeding, at least in England', and added that if 'it was thought irrelevant to print the laureate's name on the bills for the performance of his plays during the Restoration period' then playwrights' names are unlikely to have been used earlier in theatrical advertising[7]. I suppose that one could get round the difficulty by arguing that *Histriomastix* need not imply a *printed* notice. Another puzzle is the fact that so many eye-witness accounts survive of productions of plays that were certainly or almost certainly Shakespeare's, over a wide span of years – not one of which bothers to mention the author's name: *1 Henry VI* (1592), *Errors* (1594), *Titus Andronicus* (1596), *Julius Caesar* (1599), *Richard II* (1601), *Twelfth Night* (1602), *Hamlet* (1607), *Othello* (1610), *Cymbeline* (1611), *The Winter's Tale* (1611), *Henry VIII* (1613)[8], etc. This cannot mean that none of the eye-witnesses knew the author's name, for *Richard II* and *Hamlet* were in print with Shakespeare's name before 1601 and 1607, and John Manningham, who wrote so discerningly about *Twelfth Night* on 2 February 1602, comparing the play with *Errors, Menaechmi* and *Inganni,* also entered a story about Shakespeare, Burbage and *Richard III* in his diary on 13 March 1602 and was certainly in touch with literary gossip. No: the eye-witnesses' silence is surprising, but to infer that the dramatist's name was not advertised or not known seems unsafe.

Be that as it may, it is clear that in the 1590s, the decade of particular interest to us, when things changed so rapidly in the theatre, at least some playwrights' names were well known. Greene and Nashe specialised in sly, glancing thrusts at literary competitors, 'in' jokes that must have been understood in London if not elsewhere. Before one of Marlowe's plays had been published Greene ridiculed 'that Atheist *Tamburlan*' as one 'bred of *Merlins* race' (1588: 'Merlin' is found elsewhere for Marlowe); Nashe excoriated that author of an early *Hamlet* as one who chose to 'imitate the Kid in *Aesop*', meaning either Thomas Kyd or one of his imitators (1589). In *GWW* Greene continued in this vein, observing the advice he himself had offered to Nashe, 'reprooue all, and name none'[9]. He seems to have assumed that, given some clues ('Shake-scene', 'by sweet S. George'), the names would be quickly guessed.

Sometimes, however, playwrights' names appear not to have been advertised in the early 1590s. That, at least, is my inference from Gabriel Harvey's remark of 1593 – 'Faith, quoth himselfe, thou wilt be caught by thy stile: Indeede what more easie, then to finde the man by his humour, the Midas by his eares ... the Play-maker by his stile ...?'[10] Shakespeare also believed that the style proclaims the poet (sonnet 76) –

> Why write I still all one, ever the same,
> And keep invention in a noted weed,
> That every word doth almost tell my name,
> Showing their birth, and where they did proceed?

– yet he took little trouble before 1598 to advertise his authorship of plays. (Perhaps he was not altogether proud of the 'public means' of his profession (sonnets 110–11), of being classed a 'rogue and vagabond' when he wanted to establish himself as 'master' Shakespeare.) At any rate it seems significant that, apart from Greene's citation of a line from *3 Henry VI*, all but two of the early tributes to Shakespeare's works before 1598 are to *Venus and Adonis* and *Lucrece*, whilst no one praised *Romeo* or *Richard III* or *Dream* – a silence that becomes more surprising the further back we push Shakespeare's start as a dramatist[11].

As I see it, we are driven to the conclusion that Shakespeare's 'breakthrough' came in two stages. The London literary world knew about him by 1592, but, except for reacting strongly to *GWW*, he himself only began to take an interest in his reputation as a dramatist in 1597, when his company allowed a 'good' text of *Richard II* to be published. (All the early texts before *Richard II* were bad, i.e. unauthorised, apart from *Titus Andronicus,* which had belonged to three different companies and thus passed out of Shakespeare's control.) The first records that identify Shakespeare as the author of named plays all belong to 1598, and it may well be that Meres' *Palladis Tamia* was the very first. (The three quartos bearing Shakespeare's name on the title-page cannot be dated more precisely than '1598'.) Meres listed twelve plays, most of which must have been outstanding successes in the 1590s: if Shakespeare's achievement as a dramatist was not widely understood before 1598, we begin to see why the public identification of so consider-able an oeuvre was bound to impress the publishers.

(II) ALLUSIONS AND REPUTATION

Having reached 1598, the year when Shakespeare became a golden name, we must now examine our task more closely. Given his contemporary impact, how is it to be measured? From contemporary allusions, we are told. It sounds reasonable, until we turn to those who have tried to carry home some of this harvest, and discover that they have too often struggled in vain. The *Shakspere Allusion-Book* is a full barn; most of the grain is there, collected by generations of scholars[12]. Attempt to sift and value the allusions, however, and you are in trouble – as can be illustrated from the partial success of E. K. Chambers and G. E. Bentley, the two outstanding authorities of this century on the Elizabethan, Jacobean and Caroline theatre. Chambers, reprinting fifty pages of 'contemporary allusions', said 'I have limited myself to passages which make some personal reference to Shakespeare', yet in fact reprinted many which make no personal reference whatever[13], that is, passages which merely name the plays, or characters from the plays or poems. If such allusions to plays and characters are to count as 'personal', many more should have been added, including authors who quote from Shakespeare. Anyone who thinks that Chambers' fifty pages reprint all contemporary allusions to 1640 is therefore hopelessly misled. Bentley saw that a little more method would not come amiss, and went too far in the other direction. Only certain kinds of allusion were to be allowed –

> an acceptable allusion must mention the name of Jonson or Shakespeare or the name of one of their compositions or characters, or it must contain at least one line quoted from their works.[14]

As reviewers pointed out, the last condition eliminates many quotations that can be considered indisputable, simply because early literary journalists and minor poets did not feel it incumbent on them to quote accurately.

As it happens, Shakespeare is probably the most quotable poet in the language. Few of the early quoters play the game according to Bentley's rules — are they then to be disregarded entirely? Take T. A.'s *The Massacre of Money* (1602) —

> Whilst that my glory midst the clouds was hid,
> Like to a Iewell in an Aethiop's eare (B2a)

— a close echo of 'As a rich jewel in an Ethiop's ear' (*Romeo*, I. 5. 43). A coincidence? In the *Shakspere Allusion-Book* (I, 111) this is the only extract cited from T. A., but we must add at least one more.

> Hast thou a hound matcht in mouth like a bell,
> Whose eares will sweepe away the morning dewe? (C3b)

Again, an inexact quotation, from Theseus' description of his hounds —

> With ears that sweep away the morning dew;
> Crook-knee'd and dew-lapp'd like Thessalian bulls;
> Slow in pursuit, but match'd in mouth like bells
>   (*MND*, IV. 1. 118–20)

According to one way of reckoning, T. A. disappears from the record of allusions; it could be urged, though, that T. A.'s ability to quote from memory places him in the front rank of early Shakespeare enthusiasts.

Bentley's wish to bring consistency to the allusion-game nevertheless deserves our thanks. Where incorrect quotation of less than a single line is concerned, we can easily lose ourselves in wishful thinking; phrases that look like echoes may be nothing of the sort, and it is difficult to know where to draw the line. So with other possible allusions not involving quotation, for example John Lane's attack on 'lewde Lecherie' in *Tom Tel-Troths Message* (1600) —

> When chast *Adonis* came to mans estate
> *Venus* straight courted him with many a wile
> *Lucrece* once seene, straight *Tarquine* laid a baite
> With foule incest her bodie to defile:
>   Thus men by women, women wrongde by men,
>   Giue matter still vnto my plaintife pen. (p. 43)

I am inclined to accept this as an allusion to Shakespeare's poems, not because the naming of the four principal characters is in itself conclusive but because Lane's book as a whole points towards 'Shakespearian' interests. Two pages later, continuing the attack on lechery, he complains of 'light-taylde huswiues' who

>   ... vnto the Banke-side roundhouse fling,
> In open sight themselues to show and vaunt. (p. 45)

This, though, is a matter of probability, not of proof.

When we move on from verbal echoes to 'situational' echoes, scenes in other men's plays that appear to be modelled on Shakespeare, method and proof are even more desirable, and impossible to find. Yet it goes without saying that a major dramatist's impact ought to be visible in the work of imitators, and that this might well be the best indication of it. While we may not wish to claim a 'school of Shakespeare', imitation there certainly was, at every level from the complete play to scenic innovations or mere technical tricks. *The Taming of the Shrew* begat, almost certainly, *The Taming of a Shrew* (1594); also Fletcher's *The Tamer Tamed* – and perhaps even some by-blow 'taming' plays such as Heywood's *A Woman Killed With Kindness*. Barnabe Barnes' *The Devil's Charter* (1607) illustrates something less familiar in its 'situational' echoes (from *Macbeth*). When Viselli has been murdered by Lucrece she '*putteth the dagger in his hand*', to suggest suicide (Act I, sc. 5); the next scene begins with a knocking from within; Barbarossa comes to fetch Viselli (as Macduff comes for Duncan), and finds him dead; Lucrece, like Lady Macbeth, is self-possessed, and then, again like Lady Macbeth, '*she soundeth*'.

No one has tried to collect and count such situational echoes, and for a good reason: it probably cannot be done. Even when there is agreement that one play influenced another, to measure this influence seems impossible. How many distinct imitations of *Hamlet* can we trace in *The Revenger's Tragedy*? The hero's character, his confidant, the closet scene, sexual nausea, the revenge theme, Yorick's skull – the list is endless. And if we despair in the case of a single play, how ridiculous to attempt to chart Shakespeare's influence on contemporary drama as a whole! Those who have studied the surviving texts (admittedly only a fraction of the original total) will still agree, I believe, that one detects conscious or unconscious borrowing from Shakespeare wherever one turns. How easy is a bush supposed a bear? Perhaps so. At present the impression cannot be quantified, and may be distorted by our greater familiarity with Shakespeare, as compared with lesser men of the same period; all the same, his impact on the art of the theatre, educating other dramatists in the use of new techniques, must have been more significant than his influence in spheres that were discussed. Contemporary poets praised his 'honey-flowing' style and his wit, but lacked a critical vocabulary to go into technical detail; contemporary dramatists, on the other hand, grasped that much more than verbal dexterity was involved. Shakespeare enriched everything he touched – dramatic structure, characterisation, the web of relationships, down to purely scenic features such as stage groupings and rhythms, or the chiaroscuro of emotion. How could professional drama-tists fail to thrill to such masterstrokes of technical inventiveness as a supposedly dead heroine's unexpected return to consciousness (Desde-mona and the Duchess of Malfi), or a dropped handkerchief?

Allusions, quotations, and 'situational' echoes need to be considered individually; each one must be related to the document in which it occurs, and to its historical context. A mere counting of allusions etc. will achieve very little, except for one kind of evidence: publication statistics. And even these statistics, to which I shall return, are probably misleading insofar as Shakespeare's 'fellows' appear to have prohibited the printing of many plays and the reprinting of others[15].

(III) CONTEMPORARY RATING

Let us now return to an earlier question – was Shakespeare rated by contemporaries 'at something like his true value'? Leaving aside the presumptuous implication that we today rate him at his true value, we can certainly piece together the jig-saw of contemporary critical comment – both favourable and unfavourable – and identify talking-points and the various levels of appreciation. Instead of assembling the evidence in chronological order, as we find it in allusion-books and most biographies, I shall divide it into different categories, which I believe will be more revealing.

1. Title-page blurbs

The publishers of play-texts sometimes picked out on the quarto title-page either characters or episodes in the play that were thought to be particularly popular. For example – 'The Second part of Henrie the fourth, continuing to his death, and coronation of Henrie the fift. With the humours of sir Iohn Falstaffe, and swaggering Pistoll' (1600); 'The Chronicle History of Henry the fift, With his battel fought at Agin

Court in France. Togither with Auntient Pistoll' (1600); 'A Most pleas-
aunt and excellent conceited Comedie, of Syr Iohn Falstaffe, and the
merrie Wiues of Windsor Entermixed with sundrie variable and pleasing
humors, of Syr Hugh the Welch Knight, Iustice Shallow, and his wise
Cousin M. Slender. With the swaggering vaine of Auncient Pistoll, and
Corporall Nym' (1602); 'M. William Shak-speare: His True Chronicle
Historie of the life and death of King Lear and his three Daughters. With
the vnfortunate life of Edgar, sonne and heire to the Earle of Gloster, and
his sullen and assumed humor of Tom of Bedlam ...' (1608). Are we to
take it that the 'low' humour of Edgar's Bedlam speeches, or of Ancient
Pistol[16], were the great attractions of these plays? We cannot wriggle
out of it by claiming that 'low' humour episodes were written for the
groundlings, since groundlings, who paid one penny to get into the
theatre, could hardly have afforded many sixpences, the cost of a quarto.
No: the stationers believed, rightly or wrongly, that well-to-do customers had particularly savoured the Pistol and 'Bedlam' scenes. The only
wriggle we can permit ourselves, if we believe that the title-page blurbs
fail to rate better things in these plays at their true value, is to urge that
the groundlings must have outnumbered the 'better sort' in the theatres,
and that vociferous applause from the pit could have been wrongly
thought to represent the general opinion.

2. Students and 'the younger sort'

Very soon after *Hamlet* first appeared, Gabriel Harvey noted in a copy of
Speght's *Chaucer* (1598) that 'The younger sort takes much delight in
Shakespeares Venus, & Adonis: but his Lucrece, & his tragedie of
Hamlet, Prince of Denmarke, haue it in them, to please the wiser sort.'
At much the same time, Part I of *The Returne from Parnassus*, a Cambridge
play, introduced a student, Gullio, who quotes briefly from *Venus and
Adonis* and *Romeo*, then adds a stanza from *Venus*, begins another, and
later exclaims rapturously, 'I'le worshipp sweet Mr. Shakspeare, and to
honoure him will lay his Venus and Adonis under my pillowe'[17]. Harvey,
with his Cambridge connections, may have seen the *Parnassus* play, in
which case we could not regard him as a completely independent witness,
but it is interesting that *Venus and Adonis* and *Romeo* were so often named
as special favourites in the sixteenth century by university men, most of
them recent graduates (W. Covell, F. Meres, R. Barnfield, J. Marston, J.
Weever, and the author of the *Parnassus* play). The wear and tear of the
original Bodleian copy of the first Folio suggests, again, that the 'younger

sort' read *Romeo* more often than any other play[18]. Is this preference for
the poem and the play surprising, or a sign of immaturity, as Harvey so
loftily implied?

3. 'The wiser sort'

Early commentators did not usually go into literary detail, so that we
cannot always be certain that praise came from genuine understanding.
Insofar as Shakespeare went his own way as a dramatist, disregarding
fashionable critical theory with its neo-classical bias, we should not expect
too much from his contemporaries – but some of them certainly
understood his uniqueness. Meres may not have meant 'Shakespeare is a
classic' when he compared him with Plautus and Seneca: he expressed
himself similarly about other contemporaries. But in 1598 Shakespeare
was only thirty-four, and the classical comparisons continued, and grew
more confident. John Davies of Hereford addressed an epigram 'To our
English Terence, Mr. Will. Shake-speare' in 1610. In the previous year
the anonymous writer of an epistle prefixed to *Troilus and Cressida* had said
of the play – 'had I time I would comment upon it . . . for so much
worth, as euen poore I know to be stuft in it. It deserues such a labour, as
well as the best Commedy in *Terence* or *Plautus*.' This is not the common
coin of literary flattery. Nor was it usual to imply, as did Heminge and
Condell in their epistle in the first Folio, that an author was so deep that
many readers would fail to appreciate him properly – another way of
saying that he needs annotation.

> From the most able, to him that can but spell: There you are
> number'd. We had rather you were weighd. Especially, when the fate
> of all Bookes depends upon your capacities: and not of your heads
> alone, but of your purses . . . we hope, to your diuers capacities, you
> will finde enough, both to draw, and hold you: for his wit can no
> more lie hid, then it could be lost. Reade him, therefore; and againe,
> and againe: And if then you doe not like him, surely you are in some
> manifest danger, not to vnderstand him.

Although we cannot know what the epistlers of 1609 and 1623 expected
readers to miss, they evidently believed that Shakespeare's plays stretched
the 'capacities' of the best. Something similar is implied, I think, by those
who testify to the wonder generated by the plays. John Weever's 'Ad
Gulielmum Shakespeare' (1599), though insecure in spelling and syntax,
left it in no doubt that thousands succumbed to the dramatist's power.

Romea Richard; more whose names I know not
Their sugred tongues, and power attractive beuty
Say they are Saints althogh that Sts they shew not
For thousands vowes to them subiectiue dutie:
They burn in loue thy children *Shakespear* het them,
Go, wo thy Muse more Nymphish brood beget them.

The *Troilus and Cressida* epistle of 1609 also commended his power (his 'power of witte, that the most displeased with Playes, are pleasd with his Commedies'), and his talent for stretching the capacity of spectators. Those who 'were neuer capable of the witte of a Commedie' found such wit in Shakespeare's comedies as 'they neuer found in them selues, and haue parted better wittied then they came'. A Latin letter of 1610, describing a performance of *Othello* by the King's men at Oxford, expatiated upon the actors' power to move in this tragedy:

Not only by speaking but also by [silent] action they drew tears [*non solum dicendo, sed etiam faciendo quaedam lachrymas movebant.*] But indeed Desdemona, killed by her husband, although she always acted her part excellently, moved us still more in her death; when lying in her bed she invoked the pity of the spectators merely by her facial expression [*ipso vultu*].[19]

Milton, in 'On Shakespear, 1630', indicated that readers felt Shakespeare's power no less than spectators.

Thou in our wonder and astonishment
Hast built thy self a live-long Monument.
For whilst toth' shame of slow-endeavouring art,
Thy easie numbers flow, and that each heart
Hath from the leaves of thy unvalu'd Book,
Those Delphick lines with deep impression took,
Then thou our fancy of it self bereaving,
Dost make us Marble with too much conceaving ...

We see therefore that the most celebrated commendation of Shakespeare, Jonson's verses 'To the memory of my beloued' contributed to the first Folio, continued rather than set the fashion. Not only did Shakespeare 'out-shine' his contemporaries, Lyly, Kyd and Marlowe, he also surpassed the best Greeks and Romans:

> when thy Sockes were on,
> Leaue thee alone, for the comparison
> Of all, that insolent *Greece*, or haughtie *Rome*
> sent forth, or since did from their ashes come.

Better than any predecessor, Jonson conveys the 'wonder' of the wiser sort.

> Sweet Swan of *Auon*! what a sight it were
> To see thee in our waters yet appeare,
> And make those flights vpon the bankes of *Thames*,
> That so did take *Eliza,* and our *Iames*!

Reflecting upon 'The applause! delight! the wonder of our Stage', Jonson publicly retracted an opinion that he had stated several times in his plays, and most recently and succinctly in his conversations with Drummond of Hawthornden – 'That Shaksperr wanted Arte'.

> Yet must I not giue Nature all: Thy Art,
> My gentle *Shakespeare,* must enioy a part.
> For though the *Poets* matter, Nature be,
> His Art doth giue the fashion.

Shakespeare's contemporaries acknowledged the power of his work, the wonder of the spectators, the sense that he excelled all predecessors. But they lacked a critical terminology that could explain his greatness – and, since he only pretended to 'small Latin and less Greek' and disregarded neo-classical models, the feeling grew that he 'wanted Arte'. Jonson, himself more guilty than anyone else in sowing this opinion, tried to make amends in the Folio verses, without success. For almost two centuries critical opinion adopted a view expressed in its most simple-minded form by John Ward, the vicar of Stratford (1662–81), 'I have heard yt Mr. Shakespeare was a natural wit, without any art at all' – until Coleridge gave it the *coup de grâce* in 1808, denouncing those who 'talk of Shakespeare as a sort of beautiful *lusus naturae*' or inspired idiot.

We may take it, I think, that Jonson changed his mind in 1623, when the Folio sheets were waiting to be bound, and he – the only contributor of two sets of verses – had the opportunity for the first time to read the texts of some of Shakespeare's master-pieces[20]. The impact of a first perusal of *Macbeth* and *Antony and Cleopatra,* of *As You Like It* and *Twelfth Night,* of *Measure for Measure* and *The Tempest* – to name only some of the most illustrious – and of the first reading of a sound text of so many plays previously available only in mangled forms, must have been astounding. We feel it in Jonson's poem – especially in its opening sixteen lines, where he adjusts to the shock that all competition with Shakespeare is useless. Jonson, so aggressively competitive, who had made a habit of publicly rebuking Shakespeare's artistic lapses, had singled out the *Henry VI* plays, *Henry V, The Winter's Tale, The Tempest,* and probably also *Julius Caesar, Twelfth Night, Macbeth* and *Pericles*[21] – all, as bad luck would have it, plays that could not be read, or read in sound texts, before 1623! The self-consciousness of Jonson's opening lines betrays an inner struggle, an acknowledgement that he is publicly committed to a different view. He seems to anticipate a possible charge of envy and 'crafty malice' (he recorded elsewhere that the players thought one of his remarks about Shakespeare 'malevolent'[22]); having disposed of that, he offers his considered judgment – that Shakespeare, while so true-to-life that he might be thought a mere copier of Nature, was nevertheless a genuine artist.

Although Jonson did not explain what he now saw in Shakespeare to make him change his mind, I find it hard to believe that an opinion he had held for so long, and so belligerently, would be given up lightly. Jonson's critical intelligence, as revealed in his *Discoveries* and elsewhere, was of the highest order: if ever anyone rated Shakespeare 'at something like his true value', and understood the magnitude of his achievement, that man must have been Jonson in 1623. Yet Jonson, we have to admit, for all his affection for 'my beloued' and critical shrewdness, failed to rate Shakespeare justly before the publication of the Folio. It follows, I think, that all the praisers of Shakespeare before 1623 were equally hampered by the absence of reading texts – a dearth not fully indicated by those who say that about half of Shakespeare's plays were printed in his life-time. So many of the printed plays were not reprinted before the Folio that we must conclude that the players sometimes made it a policy not to allow reprints – how, otherwise, can we explain these extraordinary gaps? *1 Henry IV* represents a fairly normal run of reprints for a popular book, with quartos in 1598, 1598, 1599, 1604, 1608, 1613, 1622; *2 Henry IV* appeared only once before 1623, in 1600. Can we imagine that the demand would have been so different? Other plays not reprinted before 1623 include *Love's Labour's Lost* (1598), *Much Ado* (1600) and *Troilus and Cressida* (1609), while a second group was only reprinted once, and surreptitiously, in 1619 (*Dream, Merchant, Merry Wives, Lear*). Add that readers were also misled by the grotesque inanities of the bad quartos (*Romeo, Henry V, Hamlet* etc.), and we begin to understand why it must have been next to impossible to rate Shakespeare 'at something like his true value' before 1623.

Besides Jonson at least one other contributor of verses to the first Folio amply deserves to be included with the 'wiser sort'. Leonard Digges, the step-son of the overseer (or executor) of Shakespeare's will, wrote a short poem and, probably also in 1623, a longer poem later published with Shakespeare's *Poems* in 1640, which express an independent view of some interest. The shorter one begins clumsily –

Shake-speare, at length they pious fellowes giue
The world thy Workes: thy Workes, by which, out-liue
Thy Tombe, thy name must: when that stone is rent . . .

In the second line Digges protests, I think, against the Folio publishers, who had ducked their responsibilities by giving the volume the title *MR. WILLIAM SHAKESPEARES COMEDIES, HISTORIES, & TRAGEDIES*. Jonson had issued his plays in 1616 as his *Workes*, and had been mocked for taking himself so seriously; the Folio publishers in 1623 decided not to run the same risk, and their dedication refers to the plays three times as 'trifles'. Digges, it seems, thought this wrong[23]. In the longer poem Digges put it less aggressively, and at the same time expressed his sense of Shakespeare's achievement as an artist, going beyond Jonson's claim ('Thy Art, / My gentle *Shakespeare,* must enjoy a part').

          thou hast (I will not say)
Reader his Workes (for to contrive a Play
To him twas none) the patterne of all wit
Art without Art unparaleld as yet.

Equally important, Digges tells us why he rated Shakespeare so highly, and his reasons are not quite the usual ones. Whereas earlier admirers had vaguely noted Shakespeare's 'power' (compare p. 35, above), Digges marvelled at the impact of the big scenes.

Nor shall I e're beleeue, or thinke thee dead
(Though mist) untill our bankrout Stage be sped
(Impossible) with some new strain t'out-do
Passions of *Iuliet,* and her *Romeo;*
Or till I heare a Scene more nobly take,
Then when thy half-Sword parlying *Romans* spake,

Till these, till any of thy Volumes rest
Shall with more fire, more feeling be exprest,
Be sure, our *Shake-speare,* thou canst neuer dye ...

Passion, fire and feeling gave the big scenes their unsurpassed appeal. In the longer poem Digges also pointed to the 'quarrel-scene' in *Julius Caesar* as a prime example, and indicated other favourite scenes, though only one (*Twelfth Night,* III. 4) is clearly identified. It is a fair inference, though, that he was thinking of Shakespeare's mastery of what is now called scenic form when he listed 'the jealous Moore', Falstaff and Hal, and Beatrice and Benedick.

So have I seene, when Cesar would appeare,
And on the Stage at halfe-sword parley were,
Brutus and *Cassius*: oh how the Audience,
Were ravish'd, with what wonder they went thence,
When some new day they would not brooke a line,
Of tedious (though well laboured) *Catiline*;
Sejanus too was irkesome, they priz'de more
Honest *Iago,* or the jealous Moore.
And though the Fox and subtill Alchimist,
Long intermitted could not quite be mist,
Though these have sham'd all the Ancients, and might raise,
Their Authours merit with a crowne of Bayes.
Yet these sometimes, even at a friend's desire
Acted, have scarce defraied the Seacoale fire
And doore-keepers: when let but *Falstaffe* come,
Hall, Poines, the rest you scarce shall have a roome
All is so pester'd: let but *Beatrice*
And *Benedicke* be seene, loe in a trice
The Cockpit Galleris, Boxes, all are full
To heare *Maluoglio* that crosse garter'd Gull.

It has been conjectured that Digges wrote this second poem for the first Folio, and that it was not included because it was too long. Since Digges, who died in 1635, refers to Shakespeare's 'Workes', and concentrates throughout on the plays, he must have intended the poem for the first or second Folio (1623, 1632); and the first Folio is the obvious candidate, for it is not easy to see why he would wish to repeat in 1632 his earlier remark about 'half-Sword parlying *Romans*', which had appeared in 1623. I wonder, though, whether the poem was dropped merely because it was too long. There is a better reason – Digges' tactlessness about *Catiline* and *Sejanus.* Whatever Jonson's precise role behind the scenes in 1621-23 – whether he was the Folio editor, or merely an epistler and literary adviser – he was closely associated at this time with Edward Blount, one of the two principal publishers of the Folio[24]; I suspect that either Blount or Jonson himself vetoed Digges' longer poem, which only appeared in print after Jonson's death. Did Digges, then, not know that Jonson was connected with the Folio? This is hard to credit, since Digges and James Mabbe (whose poem was printed with Digges' shorter one in the Folio) were both associated with Blount. We are driven to conclude that Digges particularly wished to set the record straight about the relative merits of the rival dramatists, perhaps because he thought Jonson capable of 'crafty malice', and suspected him of intending to use the first Folio to blow his own trumpet. To be fair he named four Jonson plays that had been performed by the King's Men – not, for example, *Epicoene* or *Bartholomew Fair* – so that it could not be countered that superior Jonson plays had suffered from inferior actors. Another explanation might be that Digges himself withdrew his longer poem when he was shown Jonson's. (In Digges' shorter poem, which probably arrived late at the printer's[25], the line 'Or till I heare a Scene more nobly take' appears to echo Jonson's 'That so did take *Eliza,* and our *Iames*'.)

(IV) SHAKESPEARE AND JONSON

We are now ready to turn to the question that has provoked more dispute than any other concerned with Shakespeare's impact – whether he or Jonson was more highly rated in the seventeenth century. G. E. Bentley, our foremost authority on the Jacobean and Caroline stage, made the case for Jonson and chose to survey the evidence for the entire century; my interest is restricted to Shakespeare's contemporary impact but, since Bentley believed that attitudes to the two dramatists remained pretty much the same throughout the whole period, it will be as well to glance at his general argument. I should say at once that, while disagreeing with Bentley here and there, I have benefited greatly from his labours and accept that Shakespeare's and Jonson's reputations are linked: Jonson's was considered unassailable by some admirers, and we disregard it at our peril.

Bentley's case may be summed up briefly, in his own words. 'Clearly, Jonson, and not Shakespeare, was the dramatist of the seventeenth century'.

Not only was Jonson mentioned oftener, quoted oftener, and praised oftener, but his individual plays and poems were named more frequently than Shakespeare's, though his canon is smaller. Only in the references to his characters does Shakespeare have anything like the unquestioned acclaim which seems to us now so inevitably his.[26]

The inference here drawn, that the number of allusions indicates the quality of 'acclaim', was challenged by reviewers. And, if numbers mean anything, did Bentley get the numbers right? He excluded publication figures, which would have weighed heavily in Shakespeare's favour –

Title-pages of a man's own works, Stationers' Register entries of those works, publishers' advertisements, and sale catalogues have all been eliminated. These are publishing records and not allusions.[27]

On the other hand, it has been said, Bentley 'jacked up' the Jonson figures by including advertisements and 'the imprints of several books "to be sold at the Ben Jonson Head"'.[28]

Without wishing to attach too much significance to figures, we may hold that some are more meaningful than others. I think that Sir Walter Greg rightly stressed the importance of publication statistics, which contradict Bentley: by 1660, 19 of Shakespeare's plays had been published separately, in 66 editions, giving an average of almost 3½ editions for each play; for Jonson the figures were 11 plays, 16 editions, an average of under 1½. As for collected editions, by 1680 'Jonson's earlier plays were printed twice, his later only once. Shakespeare's were all printed three times – say twice as often'[29]. It cost little to write commendatory verses for Jonson – after all, literary praise is often the trifling entrance fee to a mutual benefit society; but to buy a quarto cost sixpence, and the Folios must have been very expensive indeed. Purchasers of quartos and Folios may have failed to print their views about the relative merits of Shakespeare and Jonson, but they voted eloquently with their purses.

Another form of evidence not taken seriously enough by Bentley, I think, concerns surreptitious publication. Under the decade 1691–1700 he mentions that references to apocryphal plays favour Shakespeare by 28 to 7, adding, 'this figure is not very significant because of the much greater number of apocryphal plays in the Shakespeare canon'[30]. Is this 'much greater number' not itself significant? When we add together apocryphal plays, forged title-pages, bad quartos and other parasitic publications (compare pp. 45 ff.) we again learn that the demand for Shakespeare left that for Jonson far behind.

As rehearsed so far, the argument against Bentley urges that he arbitrarily included evidence that favoured Jonson and excluded evidence that favoured Shakespeare. We need not give too much time to such boundary disputes if we agree that allusions are not all equal, and that merely counting them, by whatever rules, will never yield a satisfactory answer. It is the quality of the allusion that matters; different kinds of evidence must be given more or less weight. Let us take an example – Bentley's view that 'not *Hamlet, Lear, Othello,* or *Macbeth,* but *Catiline* was the premier English tragedy in the minds of seventeenth-century writers'.[31] To support this ranking Bentley cited (i) the number of allusions (89 to *Catiline,* 40 to *The Tempest,* Shakespeare's highest-placed play); (ii) mid-century allusions that appear to rate *Catiline* above all competitors; (iii) the fact that John Cotgrave, in *The English Treasury of Wit and Language* (1655), quoted *Catiline* 33 times, 'nearly twice as often as any play of Shakespeare's'.[32]

What can be said on the other side? (i) Leonard Digges, quoted above (p. 39), reported that audiences, 'ravish'd' by *Julius Caesar,* thereafter took less kindly to *Catiline,* which they thought 'tedious (though well laboured)'; (ii) Shaftesbury, looking back in 1710, said of *Hamlet* that 'it appears to have most affected *English* Hearts, and has perhaps been oftenest acted of any [tragedies] which have come upon our Stage'[33]. (iii) Though highly praised, *Catiline* was only reprinted on average once every ten years. (Quartos: 1611, 1635 (twice), 1669, 1674; Folio texts: 1616, 1640, 1692; total: 8.) Reprints of *Hamlet* indicate a much greater demand. (Quartos: 1603, 1604–5, 1611, undated edition, 1637, 1676, undated edition, 1683, 1695; Folio texts: 1623, 1632, 1663, 1685; total: 13). I am reminded of the admirer of *Paradise Lost* who said 'I had rather praise it than read it' – a remark that throws light on commendations of *Catiline* and of Jonson in general.

Several kinds of good evidence indicate that not *Catiline* but *Hamlet* was the 'premier English tragedy' or, as George Farquhar described *Hamlet* in 1702, 'the Darling of the English Audience'[34]. *Catiline* could boast of a *succès d'estime,* whereas Shakespeare's tragedy had a wider appeal: 'Faith it should please all, like Prince *Hamlet'* (A. Scoloker, 1604).[35] The case for *Catiline,* though it usefully reminds us that not everyone rated Shakespeare as we do today, is far from proven. Can we take the Jonson-Shakespeare debate beyond a conclusion in which so little is concluded? At the very least, I think, we might in future examine the key witnesses more closely – that is, scrutinise each document in its entirety and in its historical context – instead of merely counting allusions or thumbing through allusion-books. We should then be better able to assess the weight of support for each of the two dramatists.

The importance of both the document as a whole and the context can be illustrated from Bentley's evaluation of two praisers of Shakespeare. Bentley rated Meres' paragraphs as unique – 'no other example of such unqualified enthusiasm is known during the dramatist's life-time, and none appeared at the time of his death'[36]. Yet, Bentley went on, Meres was equally enthusiastic about many other writers.

> Meres mentioned Michael Drayton more often than he did Shakespeare, and wrote more lines about his work. In his list of 'the best for Comedy amongst vs' he names sixteen dramatists besides Shakespeare, and in his list of the best for tragedy, twelve, and at least half the dramatists so praised seem very obscure to us now.

Here the counting habit reasserts itself. Leaving that aside, I am uneasy about the implication that Meres did not see Shakespeare as in a class of his own. Should he not have been included in the lists of the best for comedy and tragedy simply because inferior dramatists are named as well? Given Meres' addiction to lists, Shakespeare's inclusion amongst weaker brethren by no means indicates that Meres rated them all alike. What is truly significant is Meres' separate paragraph on Shakespeare ('As *Plautus* and *Seneca* are accounted the best for Comedy and Tragedy among the Latines: so *Shakespeare* among ye English is the most excellent in both kinds . . .'), and the fact that he listed so many of Shakespeare's plays.

Not only did Bentley underrate Meres' enthusiasm, he also thought less well than seems reasonable of another enthusiast. The writer of the epistle prefixed to *Troilus and Cressida* (1609) placed Shakespeare ahead of other dramatists ('especially this authors Commedies . . . the most displeased with Playes, are pleasd with his Commedies'), and thought him worthy of annotation, like the classics. Bentley, however, remained unimpressed: the epistle was written 'by the publisher as a device to sell his book, like the blurbs on the dust jackets of modern novels'[37]. The wish to promote sales must be conceded. Nevertheless, compared with other publishers' epistles prefixed to plays, this one is unusual. It is more confidently literary, and it is unsigned. (Epistles prefixed to plays before 1609 were usually identifiable as either the dramatist's or the printer's. Some were headed 'The Printer to the Reader', others were signed by the printer or publisher: a practice not followed in *Troilus and Cressida*). It looks much more like the work of a connoisseur who, asked to compose the usual five or six lines, seized the opportunity to vent his personal enthusiasm. The signficant fact, therefore, is not that the epistle is by the publisher (which cannot be proved) but that its tone differs so markedly from the traditional publisher's preamble.

It will be clear by now that I disagree with Bentley's reading of some of the crucial documents, and with some of his methods and conclusions. Too many good witnesses said, like Dryden in the essay *Of Dramatick Poesie* – 'however others are now generally preferred before [Shakespeare], yet the age wherein he lived, which had contemporaries with him Fletcher and Johnson, never equalled them to him in their esteem'[38]. Nevertheless Bentley's attempt to state the case for Jonson is most valuable: it reminds us that in the seventeenth century not everyone thought Shakespeare, as Matthew Arnold was later to describe him, the 'loftiest hill'. Some of Bentley's witnesses bear out Dryden's remark, 'others are now generally preferred'. As society moved towards the 'Augustans' there was a drift away from Shakespeare; it must be stressed, however, that this was largely a matter of critical fashion, not necessarily of liking or genuine comprehension. Shakespeare's artistic aims were not understood whereas Jonson was 'correct', therefore Jonson was the man to follow.

Dryden spoke for his time when he distinguished between Jonson as the literary and Shakespeare as the natural writer. Shakespeare 'needed not the spectacles of books to read Nature', he wrote 'luckily'; Jonson was 'the most learned and judicious writer which any theatre ever had'.

> Shakespeare was the Homer, or father of our dramatic poets; Jonson was the Virgil, the pattern of elaborate writing; I admire him, but I love Shakespeare.

If Dryden here echoed Mulcaster's famous sentence ('I love Rome, but London better ... I honour the Latin, but I worship the English'), this would be in line with the now general feeling that Jonson stood for the classics (admirable), whilst Shakespeare represented the native tradition. A similar feeling may be reflected in an aside by Milton, which cannot count as an 'allusion' even though Shakespeare must have been in his mind: '*Aeschulus, Sophocles,* and *Euripides,* the three Tragic Poets unequall'd yet by any, and the best rule to all who endeavour to write Tragedy' (Preface to *Samson Agonistes,* 1671). This from Milton, who had once expressed himself so unreservedly about 'my Shakespeare' and his native wood-notes wild!

Tastes were changing. Bentley, though he printed so many new 'allusions', devised a method of assessing literary reputation that charted some fluctuations of taste but disregarded much of the crucial evidence. In particular, Dryden's informed opinion, apparently based on discussions with older men who were living witnesses. Looking back, Dryden in 1668 divided Shakespeare's 'reputation' into three phases. The first, the 'age wherein he lived', never equalled Jonson or Fletcher to Shakespeare; the third saw a decline ('others are now generally preferred'); in between came the reign of Charles I:

> in the last King's court, when Ben's reputation was at highest, Sir John Suckling, and with him the greater part of the courtiers, set our Shakespeare far above him.

It is surely significant that the decline only set in after the closing of the theatres. Until then, for about thirty years from Shakespeare's retirement, the 'wonder and astonishment' of ravished audiences continued. This posthumous admiration is itself noteworthy, compared with the usual rapid demise of an author's popularity after his death: it confirms what we are told by Francis Meres, John Davies, Anthony Scoloker, the *Troilus and Cressida* epistle, Thomas Freeman, William Basse, Digges, Jonson, Heminge and Condell, and others – that already in his own lifetime Shakespeare impressed contemporaries as a classic.

(V) SURREPTITIOUS PUBLICATIONS

The most unambiguous evidence of Shakespeare's pre-eminence in his life-time is to be found in the exceptional number of surreptitious publications based on his plays. Before the introduction of modern copyright, surreptitious publication was the highest form of flattery, a clear indication that a book or author was in demand. At the beginning of this century A. W. Pollard knew of only four 'piratical' (or unauthorised) texts, the 'bad quartos' of *Romeo* (1597), *Henry V* (1600), *Merry Wives* (1602) and *Hamlet* (1603). Peter Alexander, in the 1920s, added *The Contention* (1594) and *The True Tragedie of Richard Duke of Yorke* (1595), piratical texts of *Henry VI*, Parts 2 and 3; *Richard III* (1597), *King Lear* (1608) and *Pericles* (1609), though they differ in some respects from other bad quartos, are widely thought to belong to the same category; and *The Troublesome Raigne of Iohn* (1591) and *The Taming of A Shrew* (1594) have also been added to the list, either as bad quartos or as derivative plays closely modelled on Shakespearian originals. Of the last two only *A Shrew* can be said to have won fairly general recognition as a bad quarto[39]; without making too much of doubtful cases, therefore, we can summarise current thinking as follows: agreed bad quartos, six; possible bad quartos, eleven. Compare these figures with Leo Kirschbaum's 'A Census of Bad Quartos'[40] and we discover that no other dramatist was honoured by surreptitious publication to anything like the same extent. Kirschbaum in 1938 assigned nine to Shakespeare, and two to Robert Greene, his nearest rival; since 1938 more 'bad quartos' have been identified, but Shakespeare remains far ahead of the rest of the field.

False attributions tell the same story. As soon as publishers grasped that Shakespeare's name helped to sell books, they naturally placed it prominently on title-pages; the obvious next step was that unscrupulous men used his name to sell plays that, as all the world now agrees, could not have come from his pen. Here is a list of plays falsely ascribed to Shakespeare in his life-time, or given his initials, together with the names of printers and publishers. 1. *Locrine* (1595). 'By *W. S.*' Printed by Thomas Creede. 2. *Thomas Lord Cromwell* (1602). 'Written by W. S.' Printed for W. Jones. 3. *The London Prodigal* (1605). 'By *William Shakespeare*'. Printed by T. C. for N. Butter. 4. *The Puritan* (1607). 'Written by W. S.' Printed by G. Eld. 5. *A Yorkshire Tragedy* (1608). '*Written by* W. Shakspeare'. Printed by R. B. for T. Pavier. 6. *The Troublesome Reign of John King of England* (second edition, 1611). 'Written by W. Sh.' Printed by V. Simmes for J. Helme. (Third edition, 1622, 'Written by W. Shakespeare'.)

Deliberately false attributions were very rare before the closing of the theatres. Forged title-pages were even more unusual. Three years after Shakespeare's death, however, two stationers decided to publish a collection of his plays, ran into trouble and tried to extricate themselves by forging title-page dates. William Jaggard (who later printed the first Folio) and Thomas Pavier in 1619 reprinted ten plays, five of which they falsely dated 1600 or 1608, as if to suggest that they were merely selling off old stock. It is thought that Pavier was the moving spirit behind this venture, as Jaggard, who had been blind for some years, made Pavier the overseer of his will, and no doubt depended on him; in addition, Pavier owned the 'copyright' of five of the ten plays. Although Pavier apparently tried to conceal himself by putting exceptionally short imprints on the title-pages, giving not his full name but only his initials, 'T. P.', the King's Men knew what was happening and were not amused. Five of the ten plays were 'bad quartos' and two were not by Shakespeare at all. The Lord Chamberlain (William, Earl of Pembroke, dedicatee of the first Folio in 1623) wrote to the Stationers' Company on 3 May 1619, on behalf of the King's Men, directing that none of their plays should be printed without their consent.

The mystery of the 'Pavier quartos' was first solved by brilliant bibliographical detective-work some three hundred years later[41]. It proves Pavier to have been sufficiently convinced of the selling-power of Shakespeare's name to be willing to take considerable risks — a point of some relevance to another group of 'Shakespearian' publications which I shall call the Shakespeare novels.

That the popularity of plays sometimes inspired the writing of parasitic literature is not surprising. Ballads are believed to have followed hard upon success in the theatre (John Danter entered *Titus Andronicus* and also 'the ballad thereof' in the Stationers' Register on 6 February 1594). It is likely that H. M.'s translation of Jean Du Bec-Crespin's *Historie of the Great Emperour Tamerlan* (1597) was similarly prompted by a theatrical triumph, although H. M. does not mention the play. Such attempts to take advantage of popular interest in a play's story remained rare, however, until the year 1608, when four such publications were registered or issued, an unprecedented event. Two of the publishers' names are of special interest. (1) *The Hystorie of Hamblet.* Printed by R. Bradock for T. Pavier. (2) *The Historie of Titana, and Theseus,* by W. Bettie. Printed by T. C [reede] for T. Pavier. (3) *The Painfull Aduentures of Pericles Prince of Tyre,* by George Wilkins. Printed by T. P. for N. Butter. (4) *The Life and Death of the Merry Devill of Edmonton,* by T. Brewer (1631; SR entry, 5 April 1608). Printed by T. P [urfoot] for F. Faulkner. The first, a translation from P. de Belleforest's *Histoires Tragiques,* includes details not in Belleforest that clearly derive from the play (notably Hamlet's cry, 'A rat, a rat' as he thrusts his sword into 'the hangings' in the closet-scene). The third contains an epistle begging the reader to accept the novel in lieu of the play (which appeared as a 'bad quarto' in 1609) — 'intreating the Reader to receiue this Historie in the same maner as it was vnder the habite of ancient *Gower* ... by the Kings Maiesties Players excellently presented.' Of the second, a rambling prose romance that combines the story of Theseus with the 'coast of Bohemia', pirates, the Landgrave of Hessen etc., it need only be said that 'Titana' is a young lady totally unknown to Greek mythology, and that Shakespeare first suggested the love of 'Titania' and Theseus (*MND* II. 1. 76), a hint blown up beyond one reader's endurance by the good W. Bettie. The fourth, Brewer's *Merry Devill,* has only a remote connection with the anonymous play of the same name (first acted in 1603 or 1604) which was performed by Shakespeare's company and was later ascribed to his authorship[42]. Two of the 'Shakespeare novels' were manifestly published because of the popularity of *Hamlet* and *Pericles;* a third, it seems, because the names Titana and Theseus might lure admirers of *A Midsummer*

Night's Dream; the fourth again followed a play that was a great favourite, one that at some stage before 1653 acquired a 'Shakespearian' label.

Pavier's name catches the eye first. He not only published *Hamblet* and *Titana and Theseus* in 1608, he also put out *A Yorkshire Tragedy* in the same year as '*by* W. Shakspeare'. And N. Butter is another possible villain: he issued *The London Prodigal* in 1605 ('By William Shakespeare'), the prose *Pericles* in 1608, and also the *King Lear* of 1608, a text widely thought to have had a surreptitious origin[43]. What are we to make of this? It looks as if the Shakespeare 'novels' were part of a large-scale campaign in 1608 by unauthorised persons to take advantage of the dramatist's extraordinary popularity. In addition to the novels, the year saw the publication of *A Yorkshire Tragedy* and *King Lear*, 'blocking' entries in the Stationers' Register for *Pericles* and *Antony and Cleopatra*, to prevent publication (20 May); and there was some carry-over into 1609, the year of the play *Pericles* ('bad quarto'), of *Troilus and Cressida*, published against the wishes of 'the grand possessors', and of the *Sonnets*, a collection withheld from publication for some time, lacking an author's dedication and almost certainly printed without his consent.

Why such unusual activity in 1608–9, and so much of it clearly unauthorised? Early in the reign of James I, according to Chambers, Shakespeare must have had his headquarters in London, though 'more free than of old for occasional sojourn in Stratford'; by 1610 at the latest, however, Stratford had become his permanent home[44]. The fact that stage-directions in *Coriolanus* (*c.* 1608) are more elaborate than those in *Antony and Cleopatra* (*c.* 1607) suggests that Shakespeare expected to be absent during the period when *Coriolanus* would be rehearsed. Either he had already settled in Stratford or this was a year of longer absences from London: the Paviers and Butters saw their chance, and the novels, a falsely attributed play and several bad quartos rapidly succeeded one another[45].

Apart from Pavier and Butter, a third and more respected name must be added to the list of daring rogues. William Jaggard, mentioned above, brought out *The Passionate Pilgrim* in 1599 as 'By W. Shakespeare' – a small volume of twenty short poems, several of which are certainly by other poets; to fill out this flimsy collection he added poems by Heywood to the third edition of 1612, whereat, we hear, Shakespeare was 'much offended'; he participated in the 'Pavier quartos' of 1619; and from about 1620 he invested time and money in that very expensive gamble, the first Folio, a venture that dragged on for so long and tied up so much capital that it could easily have led to bankruptcy. In different ways, and over a period of twenty-four years, Jaggard embodies the faith of the stationers in William Shakespeare, whose plays were so highly prized that they prompted surreptitious and parasitic publications, and false ascriptions, on an unparallelled scale. The stationers were well aware of Shakespeare's unrivalled popularity, and did not need to be told, in the prophetic words of the *Troilus* epistle, 'when hee is gone, and his Commedies out of sale, you will scramble for them, and set vp a new English Inquisition'.

(VI) SHAKESPEARE'S ATTITUDE

Finally, a word about Shakespeare's own attitude to his literary reputation. G. E. Bentley expressed the orthodox view:

he did not himself take to the printers any of the plays he wrote for the Lord Chamberlain-King's company. When his plays were published they appeared without any indication of the author's sponsorship – no dedications, no epistles, no addresses to the readers, no commendatory verses from friends ... So many scores of obvious errors [are found] in all the quartos that one can be sure that no author proofread the sheets at the printing house. Nor can it be hypothesized that the numerous errors may derive from an author who really *was* interested in the publication of his plays, but who was temperamentally careless about the dull chore of proofreading. This cannot have been the temperament of William Shakespeare, for he did take great pains with his text when he published his poems.[46]

As I have suggested elsewhere[47], this traditional view fails to account for some of the facts. The issue of Shakespearian good quartos to replace 'bad' texts (*Romeo*, 1599; *Hamlet*, 1604–5; probably *Love's Labour's Lost*, 1598) must have had the author's approval, at the very least, he being a leading 'sharer' in his company; more likely, though, Shakespeare himself requested the publication of these good quartos. It was understood that bad texts brought about 'the iniury and disgrace of the Authors'; and many other bad quartos were published, yet good quartos replacing the bad are almost unheard of (*Philaster*, 1622, is the only really similar case). Shakespeare, like Fletcher, had enough 'pull' with his fellows to insist on good quartos, to heal his injured reputation; we hear that he was 'much offended' by one surreptitious text – so it is hard to resist the conclusion that he was personally responsible for the good quartos.

Why, then, did he supply no dedications or epistles for the quartos?

Dedications were not customary before 1607. Francis Burton, the publisher of *The Tragedy of Tiberius* (1607), could recall 'but a singular President' for the dedication of a play:

> the reason wherefore so many Plaies haue formerly beene published without Inscriptions vnto particular Patrons (contrary to Custome in diuulging other Bookes) although perhaps I could nerely guesse yet because I would willingly offend none, I will now conceale.

The only Shakespearian good quarto to come out after 1607, *Troilus and Cressida*, was published against 'the grand possessors wills', i.e. was unauthorised; Shakespeare's failure to provide dedications for the other good quartos, in short, was not only not surprising – it was the normal procedure at the time.

What of the difference between the textual lapses in the play-quartos and the careful printing of the poems? Bentley confused the issue by not comparing like with like. Had he selected play-texts by other dramatists (excepting Jonson, a special case), it would have emerged that, even when armed with authorial epistles etc., they could boast just as many 'obvious errors' as Shakespeare's. The poor quality of the printing of play-texts, discussed long ago in a brilliant paper by R. B. McKerrow[48], was not an isolated phenomenon, and obvious errors in good quartos tell us little about the author's 'interest'. On the other hand, Shakespeare's poems – written at a time when the plague threatened his theatrical career – naturally called for every care, being 'the first heir of [his] invention' in narrative poetry, his first signed publication, and, last but not least, his first overture to an influential patron.

Elizabethan dramatists said of their plays that 'the life of these things consists in action' (Marston), i.e. in performance, which was considered a form of publication; Beaumont actually called the first edition of *The Faithful Shepherdess* a 'second publication'. The absence of dedications, epistles etc. from Shakespeare's good quartos, and the presence of some obvious errors, is not so significant when this is recalled: the reputation of a play had to be made in the theatre, and the printed version counted as a poor second-best. So with the dramatist: Shakespeare's reputation, acquired in the theatre, was safe; no special efforts were therefore necessary when one of his play-texts went to the printer's – it was treated like any other play.

Shakespeare's attitude to his reputation as a dramatist remained the same throughout his career. His early plays came into print without his name, though it would have been easy for him to have it put on the title-

page, had he wished; about half of his plays were not printed in his life-
time; and the good quartos were sent into the world without flourishing
epistles or the like, in the ordinary way of business. Perhaps, as he
prospered, he found it awkward to combine the roles of professional
dramatist and property-owning 'gentleman'; although a few dramatists
were described on title-pages as 'Gent.'[49], those who wrote for the public
theatre were a rough lot, many of them deplorably familiar with the
insides of prisons. Francis Meres, while probably inaccurate in some
points of fact, correctly conveyed the public 'image' of the professional
playwright when he said 'As *Anacreon* died by the pot: so *George Peele* by
the pox . . . *Robert Greene* died of a surfet taken at Pickeld Herrings, &
Rhenish wine . . . *Christopher Marlowe* was stabd to death by a bawdy
Seruingman, a riuall of his in his lewde loue'[50]. A gentleman might write
and publish poetry, but no real gentleman could stoop to write for the
public theatre. One scrap of evidence that survives and high-lights the
chasm between the two worlds is the York Herald's complaint of 1602
that the Garter King-of-Arms had granted arms to unsuitable persons,
including 'Shakespear ye Player'[51].

Nonetheless, while Shakespeare did not often solicit notice by
publishing his plays individually, he may well have planned a collected
edition. Heminge and Condell seem to say so –

It had bene a thing, we confesse, worthie to haue bene wished, that the
Author himselfe had liu'd to haue set forth, and ouerseen his owne
writings; But since it hath bin ordain'd otherwise, and he by death
departed from that right, we pray you do not envie his Friends, the
office of their care . . .

The opening of Leonard Digges' Folio verses also suggests that a long-
standing pledge has at last been honoured ('*Shake-speare*, at length thy
pious fellowes giue / The world thy Workes'). We need not suppose
Shakespeare to have been completely indifferent where his reputation was
concerned, even if in general he willingly accepted his colleagues' wish to
keep the company's plays out of print for as long as possible.

Shakespeare's attitude to his own work was not too unusual by
Elizabethan standards. What I find astonishing is that, in an age when
writers so frequently adorned their books with complimentary verses
addressed to them by their friends, not a single such poem survives from
his pen. Can we suppose for a moment that he was never asked? One
could of course cultivate one's own literary reputation by adoring a rising
star, or by attaching oneself to a clique: he chose not to do so, presumably

because he thought his reputation secure. All the more interesting, therefore, that he did bring himself to compose *The Phoenix and Turtle,* a poem signed 'William Shake-speare' in Robert Chester's *Loves Martyr* (1601). In this poetical collection Chester celebrated the love of Sir John Salisbury (the phoenix) and his wife (the turtle), and the offspring of this love, their daughter; he also prevailed on Jonson, Chapman, Marston and others to contribute verses. Shakespeare's poem, as Chambers dryly commented, 'cannot rest upon any deep study of Chester's work, since it laments the childless death of the phoenix and turtle'[52] – which suggests that the only 'complimentary' poem from his pen was not a voluntary offering but was written to order. Is it not in character, then, that one so disinclined to compliment others in public also refrained from decking out his plays with epistles and addresses to the reader?

3
Shakespeare's First Plays

(I) 'LATE START' OR 'EARLY START'?

By 1592, when Greene described him as 'in his owne conceit the onely Shake-scene in a countrey', Shakespeare had already established himself in London. Two years later R. B. explained what had happened, less emotionally, in *Greenes Funeralls*:

> Greene, is the pleasing Obiect of an eie:
> Greene, pleasde the eies of all that lookt vppon him.
> Greene, is the ground of euerie Painters die:
> Greene, gaue the ground, to all that wrote vpon him.
> Nay more the men, that so Eclipst his fame:
> Purloynde his Plumes, can they deny the same?

(*OED,* ground, 6b: in painting or decorative art, a main surface or first coating of colour, serving as a support for other colours; viz. Greene supplied the *ground* for all who *wrought* upon him). R. B. confirms Greene's own complaint – that by 1592 Shakespeare had eclipsed Greene, whose importance as a writer in the late 1580s had been second to none.[1]

How long did it take Shakespeare to achieve such a commanding position, not only eclipsing one man who 'pleasde the eies of all that lookt vppon him' but, according to Greene, also threatening three other popular dramatists (Marlowe, Nashe, Peele) with the same fate? The question is not easy to answer because it carries us back into the 'lost years' – the seven years between 1592 and 1585 (when Shakespeare's twins, Hamnet and Judith, were baptized on 2 February). During these seven years Shakespeare disappears from view, re-emerging in London as the darling of 'those Puppets' the actors, who, if we may believe Greene, put all their faith in him, neglecting other writers. Was it all done in a couple of years, as is widely supposed, or did Shakespeare begin his career as a dramatist in the 1580s?

There are two different views. The orthodox 'late start' chronology assigns Shakespeare's first plays to the year 1590–91, with five plays in the first three seasons: 1590–1, *2 Henry VI, 3 Henry VI*; 1591–2, *1 Henry VI*; 1592–3, *Richard III, Comedy of Errors*[2]. Believers in the 'late start' chronology accept, it seems, that in 1592, when Greene saw him as 'in his owne conceit the onely Shake-scene in a countrey', Shakespeare had written no more than three to five plays – perhaps just three or four history plays. This is of course possible; the impact of *Richard III*, at least, must have been well above the ordinary. Early allusions, however, do not prove *Richard III* to have out-distanced *Tamburlaine* as an immediate popular success; and if Shakespeare really had not brought out more than three to five plays by 1592, Greene's idea that Marlowe will suffer an eclipse similar to his own seems a little premature. Greene, of course, was less interested in accuracy than in damaging a professional rival, but his sense of Shakespeare's importance seems extraordinary if the rival had produced so little.

So we come to the alternative – the 'early start' chronology, which dates Shakespeare's first play two or more years before 1590. At first glance the difference between 'early start' and 'late start' may seem trivial. Push back the first plays three or four years, thin out the plays that immediately follow them, and the rest of the chronology survives intact. But it is not quite so simple: if the first plays are moved back into the 1580s, those of the middle period are also affected, and about half the canon must be re-dated. Nor can Shakespeare's plays be considered in isolation from Elizabethan drama in general, since some of Shakespeare's are thought to be influenced by contemporary works, and vice versa. The dating of Shakespeare's first plays, therefore, has far-reaching implications for students of the period – not least, the question whether Shakespeare was a leader or a follower of fashion.

In considering the 'early' and 'late start' chronologies I am struck first of all by Shakespeare's age. By 1590 he would have been twenty-six. All the surviving evidence suggests that he was a remarkably fluent writer ('what he thought,' said Heminge and Condell, 'he vttered with that easinesse, that wee haue scarce receiued from him a blot in his papers'); and fluent writers usually discover their talent early, and start young. Is it really conceivable that he remained unaware of his special gift till he was twenty-six? Spenser published visions and sonnets at the age of seventeen, Chatterton had completed his life's work and committed suicide at seventeen. And Shakespeare? The fact that he married at eighteen, and that he had won a leading position in the theatre at twenty-eight, suggests that he was not a late developer – rather the contrary. Could it be that he looked upon plays written before 1590 as juvenilia, and best forgotten? That is possible; but biographers and critics have long been agreed that the early histories and early comedies, together with *Titus Andronicus,* should be seen as 'apprentice-work', when the author was learning his trade 'in the work-shop.' If they are right we need not postulate earlier, lost plays. Are we to suppose then that a dramatist who wrote with such extraordinary 'easinesse', who appears to have been endowed with an exceptional quickness of wit and invention and to have been in other respects precocious, composed his juvenilia in his late twenties?

It seems inherently unlikely. How is it, in that case, that the 'late start' chronology still survives? The reason is not hard to find: the last full-scale re-examination of the chronology of Elizabethan drama and of Shakespeare, completed in 1930 when E. K. Chambers added the two volumes of *William Shakespeare* to the four on *The Elizabethan Stage,* has daunted almost all who followed. Many of Chambers' dates and assumptions have been proved wrong by later scholars, as I shall shortly show, yet no one has had the necessary time – between a quarter and a half century, at a rough guess – to dismantle the old chronology, throw out all the time-worn nuts and bolts, most of them inherited from the eighteenth or nineteenth century, collect all new facts and, finally, reassemble the whole complicated structure, – and so we continue to put up with the Chambers chronology. (How Chambers himself found time to write his monumental volumes is another story. Though Second Secretary at the Board of Education, he spent his days at the British Museum, toiling at his books. Dover Wilson described Chambers' strange way of running his department in *Milestones on the Dover Road* and, even more amusingly, in private conversation. '*The Elizabethan Stage* was a great work, a work not to be underrated. It set back the cause of English education by twenty-five years.' Did Chambers' colleagues know what he was up to? One of them, a very old and very senior ex-civil servant said to me in 1950, on hearing that I had just completed a dissertation on the chronology of Shakespeare's plays (in which, as it happened, Chambers was mentioned not infrequently) – 'My friend Eddie Chambers once wrote a little book on Shakespeare. Do you know it? Is it any good?' Pause. 'Yes,' I said, carefully, 'it's ... it's *quite* good.' My answer pleased neither of us; we eyed each other uneasily.)

The 'late start' chronology survives because few academics care to contemplate a research-project that they may never live to finish, and because civil servants are now expected to give a little of their time to their departments. Nevertheless, one man undertook a survey of Elizabethan drama – not quite on the same scale as Chambers, though still devoting many years to his task. F. P. Wilson continued work on his volume in the *Oxford History of English Literature* after he retired, and left it unfinished when he died, but was an acknowledged master in his field, one of the very few specialists of the present century whose knowledge of Elizabethan drama could be said to rival that of Chambers. And Wilson, having pondered the claims of the 'late' and the 'early start' chronologies, gave an open verdict. 'The fact is that the chronology of Shakespeare's earliest plays is so uncertain that it has no right to harden into an orthodoxy'[3]. The 'late start' orthodoxy could no longer pass without question.

That was thirty years ago. Since then more and more students of Elizabethan drama have expressed dissatisfaction with the 'late start' chronology without, however, winning general assent for a new orthodoxy: the chronology of Shakespeare's early plays, it is fair to say, remains uncertain. Must it continue so? In this chapter I shall try to re-state the case for the 'early-start' chronology, which I think much stronger than some half-hearted supporters have allowed. And I shall begin with what has become a central issue in the debate – the mysterious relationship of the two King John plays.

(II) THE TWO KING JOHN PLAYS

The relationship of *The Troublesome Raigne of Iohn King of England*, an anonymous play published in two parts in 1591, and of Shakespeare's *King John* (hereafter *TR* and *KJ*), has now been disputed for some fifty years. J. S. Smart and Peter Alexander first suggested that *TR* was not the source of *King John*, as all the text-books had it, but was itself modelled on Shakespeare's play[4]. It was a bold suggestion, for it assumed not only that *King John* could be dated five or six years earlier than was customary but that at least all of Shakespeare's 'apprentice' plays, perhaps a dozen or more, could be moved back several years. The New Arden editor of *King John* (1954), who happens to be the present writer, examined the new hypothesis and agreed that *TR* was probably the later play; and W. H. Matchett, the Signet editor (1966), came to the same conclusion. Reviewers of the two editions and other writers have, however, generally preferred what I shall call the traditional theory (that *TR* was the source of *King John*), partly, I think, because misunderstandings were not challenged and therefore acquired the status of unassailable facts. I propose to comment on some of the misunderstandings, and then to look more closely at the two plays.

Bad quarto or derivative play?

If *TR* followed *King John,* for what purpose was it written, and what kind of text is it? T. M. Parrott thought that 'if it is, as the [New Arden] editor insists, a bad quarto of Shakespeare's play, we would expect to find many of his lines and phrases reproduced, badly perhaps, in *TR* . . . but none such has been detected.' Others also stated that *TR* had been called a 'bad quarto'[5] – not surprisingly, perhaps, since the New Arden Introduction referred to 'recognized "bad quarto" characteristics' in *TR*. Nevertheless, a clear distinction was made in the Introduction between 'bad quartos', where the intention seems to have been to reconstruct a popular play as accurately as possible and to pass off the resulting text as the true original, and 'derivative plays', where, inspired by another man's success, the writer strikes out on his own and sees himself as an independent dramatist rather than as purloiner of someone else's lines. In derivative plays some 'bad quarto characteristics' may be found, but derivative plays differed fundamentally from bad quartos in not aiming at word-for-word fidelity, and Parrott misunderstood the New Arden argument in confusing the two kinds of text.

But, it may now be said, what is the evidence for 'derivative plays'? Can you prove that they existed? Three plays, all probably acted by the Queen's men and published 1591–4, are the evidence: *TR* (1591), *The Taming of A Shrew* (1594) and *The True Tragedie of Richard the Third* (1594)[6]. It matters not at all whether these three plays followed Shakespeare's *King John, The Taming of the Shrew* and *Richard III*, or preceded Shakespeare's versions: either the Queen's men's plays or Shakespeare's followed plays with similar titles, closely imitated their predecessors in their plot or in parts of it, without attempting word-for-word reconstruction. Each one of the later group has a special relationship with another play, but none can be regarded as a 'bad quarto': one way or the other, 'derivative plays' existed in the early 1590s.

The date is important. How incredible, it has been said, 'that hack writers who were so well acquainted with Shakespeare's play as to follow it scene by scene could reproduce none of the actual dialogue'[7]. Such a statement (about *TR*) assumes that hack writers would naturally aim to produce bad quartos at a date when bad quartos were entirely unknown[8]: the first bad quartos were published in 1594, and there is no evidence that 'bad quarto' reconstructions existed as early as 1591, the publication date of *TR*. It is also worth noting that most of the surviving bad quartos are piracies of plays by well-known dramatists: a bad quarto was in effect a sign that the dramatist has arrived. If *King John* could be dated as early as 1590–91 (a point to which I shall return), Shakespeare had not yet acquired a magic name, and a hack writer might think that he could do as well as, or even better than, the unknown dramatist. In short, we are not entitled to assume that the author of *TR*, supposing that this play followed *King John*, would wish to reproduce Shakespeare's actual dialogue.

Obscurities and inconsistencies. It has been fashionable for many years to argue that inconsistencies and obscurities in the 'later text' (whether *King John* or *TR*) could be explained as resulting from its dependence on the 'earlier text'. The 'obscurity' argument has weighed as heavily as any, and deserves special attention. To take a recent example, Kenneth Muir believes it impossible that *King John* preceded *TR* because

> there are some obscurities in Shakespeare's play which can be elucidated by reference to *TR*. This is not because the anonymous author made plain what Shakespeare had left obscure, but because Shakespeare cut out some connecting links.[9]

Muir cited three examples:

(i) (*KJ* ii. 1. 134ff.) Some of Shakespeare's audience would know the story about the lion-skin, but could they be expected to know why the Bastard was annoyed at the betrothal of Blanche to the Dauphin? In *TR* the Bastard is given a long speech when he sees his 'Father's foe clad in [his] Father's spoyle'; (i. 557) Blanche hints that she will love him if he wins back the lion-skin; and the Bastard later reproaches the Queen because she had half-promised that he would marry Blanche. Surely the only probable explanation of Shakespeare's obscurity here is that he was condensing the earlier play.

(ii) (*KJ* iv. 2. 1ff.: John's second coronation.) In *TR* John is given more than twenty lines (i. 1538–60) of somewhat evasive explanation, but it is apparent, though not in Shakespeare's play, that the King thinks that Arthur, who had the stronger claim to the throne, has been murdered.

(iii) (*KJ* v. 6. 23ff.) The anti-papal and anti-monastic bias of *TR* makes the motives of the Monk who poisons John easy to understand. Shakespeare eliminates much of the anti-monastic propaganda, including the Decameronian scandal of i. 1181–288 (which he presumably found distasteful) and thereby obscures the Monk's motive.

Let us look more closely at these passages. Are they really 'obscure'? (i) Is it puzzling that the Bastard is annoyed by the Citizen's proposal that

Blanche and the Dauphin should marry? We must remember that he had already ridiculed the Citizen ('these scroyles of Angiers flout you, kings', l. 373; 'Here's a large mouth, indeed', l. 457); that the Dauphin's courtly love-speech (ii. 1. 496ff.) would scarcely appeal to one who had expressed very different views about love (i. 1. 253ff.); and that the Bastard was spoiling for a fight – in brief, his attitude to the proposal is perfectly prepared for, and in character. (iii) The anti-Catholic bias of *TR* may be greater than that of *King John,* but in *King John* it is by no means eliminated. Shakespeare reminds the audience of John's plundering of the Church several times ('Our abbeys and our priories shall pay / This expedition's charge', i. 1. 48; iii. 3. 6ff.; iii. 4. 171ff.; iv. 2. 141ff.), and made one of the play's most rousing speeches out of John's anti-papal feeling (iii. 1. 162). The motives of the Monk in *King John* are not hard to understand.

John's second coronation (ii) must be considered separately, since Shakespeare himself drew attention to this 'obscurity'. John states in *King John* that he has already explained 'some reasons of this double coronation' (the audience is not told what they are), and that others will follow later. Is this 'obscure', and suspicious? No: Shakespeare merely falls back on one of his favourite short-cutting devices – the 'I need not explain' or 'I'll tell you later' convention. We meet it again when Salisbury tells the English lords that he trusts Count Melun, 'whose private with me of the Dauphin's love / Is much more general than these lines import' (*KJ* iv. 3. 16–17), or in *Hamlet* when Claudius reminds the Danes that they know all ('nor have we herein barr'd / Your better wisdoms', i. 2. 14).

In these instances, therefore, Muir can hardly claim that there is (unintended) obscurity 'because Shakespeare cut out some connecting links': (i) and (iii) are not in themselves obscure, and (ii) belongs to a different category, as an intended obscurity. It is true that some motives appear to be clearer in *TR,* but this does not mean that the equivalent passages in *King John* are obscure: good does not cease to be good merely because better is better.

Here we come to the crux of the matter. Whichever text we believe to be 'derivative', is it likely that the derivative play would be 'clearer' in points of detail than its predecessor? If we assume that the derivative text was put together like a bad quarto, and was to be passed off as its predecessor, we would not expect the second version to be clearer than the first. If, however, the derivative play was seen by its author as an independent treatment, neither more nor less indebted to its predecessor than a history play is bound to be to its non-dramatic sources, we must not be surprised if the second author sometimes 'improves' on the first. For, as R. L. Smallwood put it –

> the author who worked first from the chronicles undertook a massive reorganization of historical material; it would not be surprising if some loose ends, mixed motives, internal contradictions, remained in his text; the playwright working second had the advantage of a much simpler dramatic source to work from and it might be expected, therefore, that it would be the later play that would be sharper in its plotting and focus.[10]

TR is sometimes clearer than *King John,* but this in itself cannot decide which came first. (Clearer, of course, need not mean dramatically superior). If, however, *King John* could be shown to presuppose 'connecting links' which are found in *TR,* as Muir believed, all argument would end. Here we must remember that two versions of the same story may include details that appear to be similar but that work quite differently. As Muir himself said elsewhere –

> We cannot properly explain the coarseness of Hamlet's words to Ophelia, both in the nunnery-scene and in the play-scene, by the fact that her prototype was a lady of easy virtue ... The simple answer to these critics who say that Shakespeare's Hamlet could never have said such things, or done such things as murder his schoolfellows, is that Shakespeare's Hamlet did, and that we ought to try and explain these things in terms of the existing play.[11]

'We ought to try and explain these things in terms of the existing play'. The same applies to *King John.* We *can* explain its so-called obscurities in terms of the existing play, and the fact that *TR* supplies other (arguably clearer) explanations is neither here nor there.

Documentary links

(i) Alice Walker stated in 1956 that 'there must be some documentary link between the two plays on the evidence of their stage directions'. She gave three examples.

>   1. Enter K. Iohn, Queen Elinor his mother, William Marshal Earle of Pembrooke, the Earles of Essex, and of Salisbury (*TR* I. 1)
>   Enter King Iohn, Queene Elinor, Pembroke, Essex, and Salisbury,

with the Chattylion of France (*KJ* I. 1)
2. Enter Pembrooke, Salsburie, Essex (*2 TR* I. 26)
   Enter Pembroke, Salisbury, & Bigot (*KJ* iv. 3. 10)
3. They summon the Towne, the Citizens appeare *vpon the walls* (*1 TR*
   ii. 191); Trumpet sounds. Enter a Citizen *vpon the walles* (*KJ* II. 1.
   200)
   Enter yong Arthur *on the walls* (*2 TR* i); Enter Arthur *on the walles*
   (*KJ* iv. 3)

Of (1) Miss Walker said

> The significant feature here is the coincidence in the order in which the
> three earls are enumerated. Further, in *TR* all are addressed by name –
> Essex repeatedly; but in *King John*, Essex speaks only three lines as the
> anonymous introducer of the Sheriff and then disappears from the text
> in favour of Bigot. How, then, could a spectator deduce from a stage
> performance of Shakespeare's play that Essex was present in this
> scene?[12]

To deal with the earls first, let us not forget a third 'document' that has
links with both plays. Since it is now agreed that both dramatists
(whichever came first) independently studied Holinshed's *Chronicles*
(1587), it is surely relevant that the first two barons mentioned in
Holinshed's life of King John are William Marshall and Geoffrey Fitz-
Peter, that is, Pembroke and Essex. (They are not called Pembroke and
Essex at this point, but are identified elsewhere by Holinshed, on pages
that Shakespeare and the author of *TR* must have read)[13]. That
Pembroke, a consistently loyal supporter of Henry II and his sons, is
usually named before the other earls in Shakespeare's stage directions[14] is
not at all surprising when we consider his importance in Holinshed – he
was a key figure in John's reign, became the general of John's army, and
after John's death brought the young Henry III to Gloucester and
proposed his succession. That Essex, John's Lord Chief Justice, is named
after Pembroke in the first stage direction in both plays is equally
unsurprising, as he was named immediately after Pembroke by
Holinshed. In sum, both dramatists presumably looked at Holinshed's
opening sentences, since they both start their plays near the beginning of
John's reign, and there found that John relied on Pembroke and Essex 'to
proclaime him king', and so they both quite naturally introduced the two
earls in the first scene. Salisbury's inclusion, again, can be explained as
resulting from the second dramatist's awareness that Salisbury will be
given a major role later in the play.

The order of the earls in (1) and (2) need not point to a documentary link between the two plays. Miss Walker's third example is more interesting. It could be sheer coincidence that the same formula is found in both plays, first *upon the walls,* then *on the walls.* (Shakespeare used both formulae in early history plays, e.g. *3 Henry VI,* IV. 7. 16, V. 1. 1.) But there is another possible explanation. In the last twenty-five years it has become increasingly clear that those who prepared the copy for Shakespeare's Folio sometimes printed from, or consulted, quarto texts. Even 'bad' quartos were used[15]. For copyright purposes *King John* was treated as identical with *TR* in 1623[16], just as bad quartos were treated as identical with good texts, and therefore it is conceivable that those who prepared the Folio version of *King John,* knowing of the existence of *TR,* consulted it, as they appear to have consulted bad quartos, when Shakespeare's stage directions were illegible, or were simply missing. It is generally agreed that *King John* was printed from the author's (non-theatrical) fair copy, and we know from other Shakespearian fair copies, and from the three pages in *Sir Thomas More,* that Shakespeare often omitted necessary stage directions.

The argument from 'documentary links' has been much exaggerated. In my opinion only (3) has any weight, and even (3) could be explained as coincidence, or as compatible with our general picture of the Folio's dependence on quarto texts.

Hubert-Citizen

In the Folio, the Citizen who speaks for Angiers appears as *Citizen* or *Cit.* from II. 1. 201 to 281, and thereafter as *Hubert* or *Hub.* Long ago Dover Wilson suggested that Shakespeare meant the Citizen and Hubert to be one and the same person, and the two became one in the New Arden edition (and, later, in the Signet and Penguin editions)[17]. Parrott approved, but noted that in the scenes in *TR* equivalent to II. 1. 201–81 in *King John* the man is *Citizen,* never *Hubert,* whereas one would expect him to be Hubert if *TR* followed *King John.* 'How then does the editor account for the speech-heading *Citizen* in *TR*?'[18]

It should be said at once that Dover Wilson's theory about the Citizen and Hubert is in no sense a necessary part of the argument about *King John* and *TR*; the theory could be mistaken, and those who believe that *King John* preceded *TR* could disown it, without prejudice to their case. Nevertheless, to 'account for the speech-heading *Citizen* in *TR*' is not difficult, if we find Dover Wilson's explanation plausible. We must recall that in Act II the man is addressed as *Citizen* in *King John* (II. 1. 362,536), not as Hubert; and also that in Act II he appears on the upper stage, and would only be partly visible: the *TR* author, therefore, could easily have failed to recognise Hubert, when he re-appeared in armour on the battle-field and was first identified by name in the dialogue of *King John* (III. 3. 19), as the person previously half-seen on the upper stage and addressed as *Citizen*. Another possibility is that Shakespeare or his colleagues finally decided against making the Citizen and Hubert one part. The Folio text, now widely held to be based on an authorial manuscript, would in that case transmit a 'first shot' later abandoned, as texts based on autographs often did[19].

Connections with other texts

It has been suggested that *TR* must have come before *King John* because the former or the latter can be dated with the help of other texts. (i) Kenneth Muir wrote in 1960 that 'it is quite impossible for *King John* in its present form to have been written as early as 1590 because it echoes Daniel's *Civil Wars*'. He expanded on this in 1977[20], arguing that Daniel's account of Flint Castle –

A place there is, where proudly raisd there stands
A huge aspiring rocke neighb'ring the skies;
Whose surly brow imperiously commands
The sea his bounds that at his proud feet lies;
And spurnes the waues that in rebellious bands
Assault his Empire and against him rise

– inspired Gaunt's death-speech in *Richard II* (II. 1) and a similar passage in *King John* (II. 1. 23ff.):

that white-fac'd shore
Whose foot spurns back the ocean's roaring tides,
And coops from other lands her islanders –
Even till that England, hedg'd in with the main,
That water-walled bulwark, still secure
And confident from foreign purposes . . .

'There are too many links between the Daniel and Shakespeare passages for them to be accidental', Muir argued. 'The use of the same image would appear to be conclusive proof of Shakespeare's indebtedness'. Muir then went on to list other 'sources' of Gaunt's speech, such as Du Bartas' praise of France, printed in John Eliot's *Ortho-Epia Gallica* (1593):

O Fruitfull *France*! most happie Land, happie and happie thrice!
O pearle of rich *European* bounds! O earthly Paradice! . . .

And Lodge's poem (printed in 1584), 'Truth's Complaint over England':

> [England] a plot of beautie braue,
> Which onely soyle, should seeme the seate to bee,
> Of Paradise, if it from sinne were free.
> Within this place, within this sacred plot,
> I first did frame, my first contented bower . . .

These 'sources' of Gaunt's death-speech have been quoted because I think
it can be shown that there was a common stock of Armada rhetoric, and
that it has a bearing on Shakespeare's 'debts' to Daniel. Here are a few
more examples:

(a) seeing how secure we slept, carelesse, reposing our selues in that
our owne strength, for that wee were *hedged in with the sea* . . . peace
and plentie flourisheth in England, and all our Land floweth with
milke and honie . . . Seeing that wee are euery way *blest* and fauoured
from aboue: that the Lorde our mercifull God maketh *ENGLAND like
EDEN, a second Paradise* . . . (R. Greene, 1589)
(b) the vowed fo-men of *this happie Ile* . . . (D. F. R. de M., 1589)
(c) At length we are arriued in Albion . . .
And hope to prosper in *this louely Ile*
. . . [Its attractions] equall it with Tempes *paradice* . . . (*Locrine, c.* 1590)
(d) His Armadoes . . . fled from the breath of our Cannons . . . . The
winds . . . raised vp high *bulwarks* of *bellowing waues,* whence Death
shot at their disordred Nauy: and the *Rockes* with their ouer-hanging
iawes eate vp all the fragments of oake that they left. So perisht our
foes; so the Heauens did fight for vs. (Nashe, 1592)
(e) England . . . thou art *walled with Seas.* (Nashe, 1593)[21]

'Happy England' and 'invincible England' rhetoric abounds in the
ephemera of the 1580s and 1590s, as also in more substantial works such
as Camden's *Britannia* (1586), and many of its phrases were echoed by
Shakespeare. That being so, it seems likely that in *King John* and *Richard II*
we have to reckon with a general indebtedness to Armada rhetoric, rather
than with direct borrowings from Eliot, Lodge, Greene, etc.; and the
'links' between *King John* and Daniel appear to belong to the same
rhetorical tradition, and to have no special significance. The extracts I

have quoted include parallels for '*hedg'd in with* the main', 'water-*walled*'
'*bulwark*' (*King John* II. 1. 26–7), and (d) gives the essence of *King John* II.
1. 23–4, 'that white-fac'd shore, / Whose foot spurns back the ocean's
roaring tides', viz. the Armada commonplace that rocks and seas
defended England because 'the Heauens did fight for us.' Muir believes
that in *King John* Shakespeare must be indebted to Daniel's 'that at his
proud feet lies; / And spurnes the waues'. Here, though, the rock that
spurns (kicks) back the waves, the underlying image in Shakespeare and
Daniel, belongs to another set of Armada commonplaces – the rock in the
ocean, an emblem of 'constancy' which, with its biblical overtones, was
adopted by Protestant England as its own emblem, representing the true
faith. 'England happie through her *Elizabeth,* sate crowned with a wreath
of peace . . . as a Rocke vnmooueable' (I. L., 1589[22]). The obverse of this
familiar idea was the boast, ascribed to Spain, that England was not a rock
but merely a mole-hill – 'this mool-hill Isle, that litle England hight';
'alas, what's *England* to the power of *spaine*? a Molehil, to be placed
where it pleaseth them' (R. W., 1590[23]). Since the foot-spurning is not
found in Holinshed, Daniel's source[24], it seems most likely that Shakespeare followed and expanded upon the tradition, here as in the rest of the
King John speech. Daniel could have been independently inspired by the
same tradition; and, of course, we must not rule out the possibility that
Daniel, while writing the *Civil Wars,* remembered a resounding passage
from *King John,* and was actually the debtor[25].

(ii) M. P. McDiarmid[26], arguing that *TR* preceded *King John,* alleged
that *TR* influenced Marlowe's *Edward II* (I. 4), where

> the Archbishop of Canterbury threatens to 'Curse' Edward and
> 'Depose him and elect another king,' if . . . Gaveston is not outlawed.
> Edward reflects that he is powerless to resist:
>
> > 'It boots me not to threat; I must speak fair:
> > The legate of the Pope will be obey'd.'
>
> . . . No chronicle suggested this representation of events. *The
> Archbishop was not legate to the Pope; there was no Papal threat to ex-
> communicate Edward.* Obviously the scene is modelled on the similar
> historical events presented in *TR* . . .

No chronicle? Holinshed wrote that

> The archbishop of Canturburie, being latelie returned from Rome, . . .
> did pronounce the said Peers [Gaveston] accursed, if he taried within
> the realme longer than the appointed time, and likewise all those that

should aid, helpe, or mainteine him[27].

The threat against all who might aid Gaveston clearly included the king, his principal friend. And if the Archbishop is not at this point called 'legate to the Pope', Marlowe, a native of Canterbury and holder of an Archbishop Parker scholarship, is likely to have known a fact recorded earlier in Holinshed – that from the time of Henry II

> the dignitie of legatship remained euer after to the archbishop of Canturburie by a speciall decree, so that they were intituled *Legati nati,* that is to say Legats borne
> [*Margin*: 'The power legantine annexed to Cant.']²⁸

An argument that builds on such shaky foundations need not detain us. And McDiarmid's other suggestions seem to me equally inconclusive, particularly the one that the author of *TR* 'industriously studied' the chronicle – a point that is not in dispute. ('The authors of both the plays evidently read up their story carefully ... Each, in fact, added many details not to be found in the other play.' *King John,* New Arden edn., p. xviii).

(III) SOME OTHER PLAYS

Supposing that defenders of the 'traditional' view of *TR* and *King John* have misunderstood some of the arguments, and have themselves brought forward arguments that are by no means final, where are we? We have reached the end of a road, but not the end of the journey. It will now be helpful to look beyond the two plays, two dots on the chronological grid of Elizabethan drama, to ask ourselves how confidently we can date each of the two and Shakespeare's early plays in general.

The Shakespeare chronology has powerfully influenced the discussion of *King John* and *TR,* though largely from the side-lines. Anyone who believes that Shakespeare's writing career began *c.* 1590, and that eight or nine apprentice plays must have preceded *King John*, will naturally not welcome the suggestion that *TR,* published in 1591, already echoed *King John*: it is inconvenient, it rocks the boat. Ever since Malone, the first systematic investigator of Shakespeare's chronology, decided in favour of the 'late start' theory (i.e. that Shakespeare began writing in 1590, not in the 1580s), the same thing has happened when a Charles Knight or Thomas Kenny or Peter Alexander proposed the alternative, an 'early start'[29]: each individual piece of evidence was brushed aside because, taken on its own, it seemed too flimsy to dislodge the established Shakespeare chronology. Take several together, however, and the weight of the evidence seems far less one-sided.

(i) In *Bartholomew Fair* (1614) Jonson ridiculed admirers of *The Spanish Tragedy* and *Titus Andronicus* as men whose judgment hath stood still 'these fiue and twentie, or thirtie yeeres', thus dating the two plays between 1584 and 1589[30]. 'One does not usually go to a dramatist for exact chronology' retort those who find this early date for *Titus* inconvenient. Perhaps so; but Jonson was less given to loose speaking than most on points of fact, and 25 or 30 years is more specific than a single round number would be, and suggests a wish to be exact. Moreover, Jonson gave the same figures in *Cynthia's Revels* (1600): 'they say, the *vmbrae*, or ghosts of some three or foure playes, departed a dozen yeeres since, haue bin seene walking on your stage heere'[31]. A few lines further on follows mention of '*the old Hieronimo*, (as it was first acted)', clearly one of the plays departed a dozen years since (i.e. *circa* 1588). Separated by 14 years, Jonson's two statements support one another. It is difficult not to conclude that, rightly or wrongly, Jonson believed *The Spanish Tragedy* to have been written in the 1580s. This date is now generally accepted, yet Jonson's equally unambiguous date for *Titus*, 1584–89, is thought to be inexact!

(ii) Although *Romeo and Juliet* is usually dated 1595 or 1596, a topical allusion suggests 1591. "'Tis since the earthquake now eleven years' says the Nurse (I. 3. 24). An earthquake shook London in 1580, and was remembered for many years, and the natural interpretation of the Nurse's line would be that eleven years have passed since 1580. Not so, said E. K. Chambers – 'this is pressing the Nurse's interest in chronology – and Shakespeare's – rather hard'[32]. Would he have thought so if the topical allusion had confirmed the 'late start', or is the Nurse's interest in chronology suspect only because it contradicts it?

A date as early as 1591 for *Romeo* would bring the early Shakespeare chronology toppling down, so it must be resisted at all costs. Here are two more examples of the same prejudice at work. (a) G. I. Duthie rejected the date 1591 because 'the earthquake that shook [the Nurse's] dovecot took place on "Lammas Eve" (i.e. 31 July) whereas the one that shook London took place on 6 April'[33]. To which we may reply that many remember the correct year of an important event, but how many remember the day of the year when eleven years have gone by? (b) According to Sidney Thomas, William Covell's *Polimanteia* (1595) referred to 'the terrible Earth-quake' of 1584. 'To at least one literate and

well-educated Englishman of the period, therefore, Shakespeare's earthquake reference would not automatically have suggested 1580'[34]. But, he
added, we cannot 'be sure that the 1584 earthquake was felt in England at
all; the only contemporary reference to it, outside of Covell, localizes it in
Geneva.' Well, minor earthquakes also occurred in 1583 and 1585, but as
far as Londoners were concerned *the earthquake* was the big one of 1580,
an event that lived on in the popular memory for many years. Witness
Edward Pond's almanac for 1604 and its 'briefe Computation of time
complete within this present yeare.1604.' –

	yeares
Since the whole heauens seemed to burne with fire.	30
Since the Deepe snowe.	26
Since the Generall Earthquake in England.	24

(iii) The 'orthodox' date for *Love's Labour's Lost* is 1594–5[35]. A good
case can be made for 1592, however: it rests on topical allusions that are
well-known and, I believe, pretty well agreed.

(a) Puns on *pierce, person, purse, penny* allude to Nashe's *Pierce Penilesse*
(July, 1592). Moth, the play's 'tender juvenal' and 'acute juvenal' (I. 2. 8,
III. 1. 60), partly represents Nashe, the young satirist who was beginning
to make his mark in London.

(b) Shakespeare adapted a joke about Nashe that was going the rounds
in London in 1592–3: 'She knew what she said, that intituled Pierce, the
hoggeshead of witt: Penniles, the tospot of eloquence . . . . She it is, that
must broach the barrell of thy frisking conceite.'

> *Hol.* Master Person, quasi pers-one. And if one should be pierced,
> which is the one? *Cost.* Marry, Master Schoolmaster, he that is likest to
> a hogshead. *Hol.* Piercing a hogshead! A good lustre of conceit . . . .[36]

Why and when would Shakespeare wish to put Nashe in his place? Oddly
enough, we know of only one definite ground for a quarrel, and it again
points to the year 1592 – the fact that Nashe was widely thought to be
the author or part-author of Greene's *Groats-Worth of Witte* (September,
1592) (hereafter *GWW*), which contained the notorious attack on
'Shake-scene'. 'I protest it was all *Greenes*, not mine nor Maister *Nashes*,
as some vniustly haue affirmed' Chettle wrote in December, 1592; yet,
though Nashe himself vigorously disowned *GWW*, others still hinted at
his authorship in 1593[37]. Shakespeare, therefore, had reason to think
himself injured by Nashe in the autumn of 1592, just after the publication

of *Pierce Penilesse,* either because he believed the rumours about Nashe's authorship of *GWW* or because Nashe was known to be the dead Greene's closest literary associate, the man most likely to have published if not written *GWW.* So Nashe had to be rapped: we know that Shakespeare or his friends acted quickly in extorting a disclaimer from Chettle by December, 1592, and the likeliest explanation of the quips about Nashe in *Love's Labour's Lost* is that they belong to the same quarrel and to the same date.

The 'orthodox' Shakespeare chronology dates *Titus, Romeo* and *Love's Labour's Lost* in 1593–4, 1594–5, 1594–5. I have suggested 1584–9, 1591, 1592, thus moving the plays back several years. The external evidence for such early dates is striking but not, of course, irresistible – and therefore it has been resisted. (Others have argued for the earlier dates in the past.) It should be noted, however, that those who have pronounced on the dates of the three plays since the last major investigation of 'the problem of chronology' (by E. K. Chambers, 1930) have generally considered only one play – that is, they have allowed the 'orthodox' chronology, with its built-in prejudice in favour of Shakespeare's 'late start', to influence their thinking, and there is usually little or no sign that they have connected the evidence for an earlier date with other plays where similar evidence points the same way. Why has this happened? Because the argument for Shakespeare's 'early start' is complex, and has never been fully assembled. Nevertheless, as F. P. Wilson realized, the 'late start' orthodoxy is by no means the ark of the covenant: 'The fact is that the chronology of Shakespeare's earliest plays is so uncertain that it has no right to harden into an orthodoxy'[38].

4
Shakespeare's First Plays (contd)

If the chronology of Shakespeare's earliest plays is as 'uncertain' as F. P. Wilson maintained[1], how is it that an 'orthodox' chronology has held the field for so long? The orthodox 'late start' chronology (according to which Shakespeare began his writing career in 1590, and not three or four years earlier) rests on assumptions that once made good sense, many of which have now been brought into question or superseded by later research. I propose, next, to examine these assumptions, their early history and their survival in the immensely influential work of E. K. Chambers.

(I) SHAKESPEARE'S 'SOURCE-PLAYS'

Edmond Malone, the only begetter of the orthodox chronology, argued in his *Dissertation on the Three Parts of King Henry vi* (1787) that Greene's *Groats-Worth of Witte* (1592) accused Shakespeare of refurbishing other men's plays, and in particular of re-writing *The True Tragedie of Richard Duke of Yorke* (1595) and passing it off as his own (i.e. as *Henry vi*, Part 3). *True Tragedie* and the other plays identified as Shakespeare's 'sources' must have been written before their year of publication but, it was thought, could not be pushed back very far because they echo or imitate earlier plays. Shakespeare's use of *True Tragedie* etc. consequently appeared to confirm the 'late start' chronology. E. K. Chambers, who took over the 'orthodox' chronology, published his *The Elizabethan Stage* (4 vols, 1923) without challenging Malone's views on the 'source-plays', then changed his mind after reading Peter Alexander's brilliant articles (1924) and book (1929). For, as S. Schoenbaum recently explained, the Smart-Alexander interpretation of *Groats-Worth of Witte* 'effectively carried the day'[2]. Chambers, in other words, already committed to the 'late start' theory in 1923, dropped Malone's theory about *Henry vi* when it was seen to be clearly untenable, but clung to the 'late start' – even though the two theories are intimately connected.

Had Chambers abandoned the 'late start' in *William Shakespeare* (1930), this would have invalidated many of the chronological conclusions of his earlier *The Elizabethan Stage*. In the upshot, he only slightly modified his earlier 'late start' chronology, which he had first enunciated in the following 'conjecture':

> Shakespeare's first dramatic job, which earned him the ill will of Greene, was the writing or re-writing of *1 Henry VI* for Strange's, in the early spring of 1592. During the winter of 1592–3 he revised *The Contention* . . . [3]

That is, Chambers pushed back the beginning of Shakespeare's writing career from 1592 to 1590: and he could hardly have moved it back further without seriously damaging his general account of Elizabethan drama in the late 1580s and early 1590s.

Only two 'source-plays' supposedly refurbished by Shakespeare now remain in the field; that is, only two of all those once cited in support of the 'late start' chronology. One is *The Taming of a Shrew* (1594) – and Kenneth Muir's cautious statement indicates that it can no longer be taken as axiomatic that *A Shrew* preceded Shakespeare's *The Taming of the Shrew*:

> Richard Hosley, in what is the most convincing contribution to a continuing debate, has argued that *A Shrew* postdates *The Shrew*, that it is a piratical version of it, and that the author responsible deliberately deviated from Shakespeare's play. . . .
>
> If we accept Hosley's arguments, as I have gradually come to do, Shakespeare must have based his play on a number of different sources
> . . . .

Thank to Peter Alexander, Hosley and others, the argument that *A Shrew* followed *The Shrew* is now widely accepted. G. R. Hibbard, in his edition of *The Shrew*, called it 'quite conclusive', and B. R. Morris, having weighed all the evidence, supports it as well in the forthcoming New Arden edition[5].

The second 'source-play' important for the Shakespeare chronology is *The Troublesome Raigne of Iohn King of England* (1591) (hereafter *TR*); it should be noted, though, that the two views about *King John* and *TR* do not carry chronological implications that are equal and opposite. (a) If *King John* preceded *TR*, this in itself would clinch the case for an 'early start'. (b) If *TR* preceded *King John*, on the other hand, this would not in itself prove the 'late start' correct, since *King John* might nevertheless be assigned to the years 1591–2, which would still be several years earlier than its orthodox 'late start' date (1595–6).

Let us take (b) first. I conclude from it that *of all the plays once regarded as Shakespeare's 'source-plays', not one now gives significant support to the 'late start' theory;* or, to put it the other way round, *Shakespeare's supposed 'source-plays', once considered the foundation upon which the 'late start' theory was built, can no longer be used as evidence against an 'early start'.*

Of (a) it need only be said at this stage that sceptics may take more kindly to the notion that *King John* could have preceded *TR* when we have examined the 'orthodox' chronology in more detail.

(II) SHAKESPEARE AND MARLOWE

It has long been fashionable to describe Marlowe as one of Shakespeare's 'predecessors.' Contemporary allusions, formerly cited in support of this view, have now been looked at again, and turn out to be less unambiguous than was previously supposed.

(a) Greene called Shakespeare an 'vpstart Crow' in 1592. Malone thought that Greene meant a 'new upstart writer' (compared with Marlowe), and Chambers agreed: 'It is a fair inference from Greene's tone that [Shakespeare] was only just taking rank as a serious rival to the University men.' Two other interpretations of Greene's words are possible, however: either that 'Shake-scene' was an actor turned dramatist, an upstart from a lower profession attempting to climb into a higher one, or that 'Shake-scene' had the impudence to compete with University men without being one himself.[6] I incline to the latter, since Nashe and Greene both lashed at the new (non-graduate) professional writers, and pointedly addressed their remarks 'To the Gentlemen Students of both Universities' (Nashe) and 'to my fellow Schollers about this Cittie' (Greene's epistle about 'Shake-scene')[7]. Even if one of these two alternative interpretations of Greene's 'upstart' were merely possible (instead of having, in Schoenbaum's words, 'effectively carried the day'), it would follow that we are not entitled to draw chronological inferences from his words.

(b) Next, Jonson's tribute to Shakespeare. Malone agreed with Farmer's opinion, 'that Ben Jonson particularly alludes in the following verses to our poet's having followed the steps of Marlowe in the plays now under our consideration, and greatly surpassed his original.'[8]

My *Shakespeare,* rise; I will not lodge thee by
  Chaucer, or *Spenser,* or bid *Beaumont* lye
A little further, to make thee a roome . . . .
For, if I thought my iudgement were of yeeres,
  I should commit thee surely with thy peeres,
And tell, how farre thou didstst our *Lyly* out-shine,
  Or sporting *Kid,* or *Marlowes* mighty line.

Place Jonson's verses in their historical context, however, and a different
'allusion' emerges. Jonson referred to a recent poem, *Basse his Elegie* –

Renowned Spencer, lye a thought more nye
To learned Chaucer, and rare Beaumont lye
A little neerer Spenser to make roome
For Shakespeare . . . . [9]

Jonson censured Basse because Chaucer, Spenser and Beaumont, though
great, are 'disproportion'd *Muses*', that is, different kinds of writer,
whereas Lyly, Kyd and Marlowe are Shakespeare's 'peeres' (i.e. equals,
fellows, all three being dramatists). Saying that Shakespeare 'out-shone'
Lyly, Kyd and Marlowe, Jonson no more implied that all three were
necessarily Shakespeare's predecessors than Basse meant to imply that
Chaucer, Spenser and *Beaumont* (1584–1616) were predecessors: Basse had
selected three great writers who were dead, and Jonson retorted with
three more appropriate writers who were also dead (in 1623). The only
chronological deduction we are entitled to draw from Jonson's verses is
that Marlowe and Shakespeare wrote in the same 'Age' and that Marlowe
died first.

(c) The earliest allusion to Marlowe as a writer occurs in 1588, whereas
the first certain allusion to Shakespeare followed four years later, in 1592.
Does that prove that Marlowe started as a dramatist before Shakespeare?
No: we must remember that in the 1580s the names of public-theatre
dramatists remained uncelebrated. As Chambers himself explained –

The fragmentary nature of the evidence makes a dramatic history of the
period extremely difficult. The work of even the best-known writers is
uncertain in extent and chronology . . . . Marlowe's authorship of
Tamburlaine is a matter of inference; it is only by accident that we
know the *Spanish Tragedy* to be Kyd's.[10]

In addition, a writer as pugnacious as Marlowe was far more likely to attract early notice than Shakespeare, who did not seek publicity (cf. p. 28). The fact that Marlowe attracted attention first by no means proves that he began to compose plays before Shakespeare.

In this section I have argued that contemporary allusions fail to support the wide-spread view that Marlowe was Shakespeare's predecessor. It was not my purpose to argue that Shakespeare was Marlowe's predecessor, but only to indicate that early allusions to the two dramatists neither contradict the 'early start' chronology nor support the 'late start' (which dates Shakespeare's first play 1590); that is, these allusions should not be used to buttress the orthodox chronology.

(III) SHAKESPEARE AND 'THE FAERIE QUEENE'

In the three parts of *Henry VI* and in *Richard III* there are passages that appear to be influenced by *The Faerie Queene,* books I–III. Spenser's book was entered in the Stationers' Register on 1 December 1589, and includes a preface dated 23 January 1589 (i.e. 1590). A. S. Cairncross noted that

> It was possible, of course, for Shakespeare to have become familiar with *The Faerie Queene* in manuscript before publication; its influence, however, not only in *3 Henry VI*, but also in *1* and *2 Henry VI* and *Richard III*, is so widespread and so general that it seems much more likely to derive from frequent reading and assimilation, that is, from the printed book.[11]

Cairncross did not mention, however, that other London writers knew *The Faerie Queene* before it was published. A stanza from the poem appeared in A. Fraunce's *Arcadian Rhetorike* (SR 11 June 1588); and Marlowe echoed Spenser in both parts of *Tamburlaine.* 'Evidently', wrote A. C. Judson in his authoritative *Life of Edmund Spenser,*

> a portion of the poem was circulating in manuscript in London. Perhaps Bryskett ... took the manuscript with him on a visit to England, where we find him in the summer of 1587. He had been deeply interested in the inception of the poem, and was later to reproach Spenser for lagging in his great enterprise.[12]

Since *The Faerie Queene* was circulating in manuscript before 1590, Shakespeare's acquaintance with the poem need not mean that the *terminus a quo* for the three parts of *Henry VI* must be 1590. From what is known of Shakespeare's assimilative powers, a single perusal of the manuscript would give him all he would want, and would be the equivalent of 'frequent reading' by lesser mortals.

(IV) FRANCIS MERES

Adherents of the 'late start' chronology have drawn strange conclusions from the list of Shakespeare's six comedies and six tragedies in Meres' *Palladis Tamia* (1598). According to E. K. Chambers 'the list is so long as to suggest that it includes all that were known to him'; hence the familiar verdict that absence from Meres' list establishes the *terminus a quo* for several plays that must date from *c.* 1598. To take one example, Chambers said of *As You Like It* that 'the entry in the Stationers' Register [1600] and the absence of the play from Meres' list of 1598 give limits of date, within which it is difficult to be more precise'[13].

Is it likely that plays already written by 1598 were omitted from Meres' list? How significant is his 'negative testimony'? No one disputes that the three parts of *Henry VI* and *The Shrew,* which are not in the list, must have existed by 1598; but these are early plays, perhaps so early that Meres had forgotten them, whereas plays usually assigned to *c.* 1598 (e.g. *As You Like It, Merry Wives, Much Ado,*) pose a more interesting problem. For if Meres' 'negative testimony' persuaded Chambers to post-date one or more plays of *c.* 1598, this must be connected with Chambers' tendency to post-date Shakespeare's very earliest plays (the 'late-start' theory).

Three years after Chambers published his conclusions, Don Cameron Allen showed that Meres' reliability as a witness had been grossly overvalued. 'Francis Meres was not a serious scholar .... Every critical statement made by Meres about an English or contemporary literary figure is imitated from the writings of Ascham, Sidney, Puttenham, Nashe, and Webbe.' Allen added, somewhat less scathingly, that

[Meres'] knowledge of his immediate contemporaries cannot be questioned, since, in many instances, they are mentioned for the first time in [Meres'] treatise. However, it can be seen that he is often doing little more than noting the current opinion on the men of his generation.[14]

Allen demonstrated that Meres' critical opinions were largely borrowed. For our purposes it is equally important to know whether or not Meres' information was up-to-date – and here I am struck by a coincidence. On the one hand it seems clear that Meres was already moving towards the Church in 1598 (he left London in 1602 to become rector of the parish of Wing in Rutland): his first book, *Gods Arithmetic* (1597) was soon followed by his translation of Luis of Granada's *Granado's Devotion* (1598). This may explain the split between an artistic and a clerical attitude in *Palladis Tamia,* the sudden intrusion of moral bias in his comments on the deaths of the most admired writers of his day, George Peele, Robert Greene and Christopher Marlowe, which I have already quoted[15]. On the other hand, Meres listed *Henry IV* as a tragedy, and appears not to have known that the play was in two parts. The coincidence that Meres, a later clergyman, already the writer of religious books, betrays imperfect sympathies with popular dramatists, at a time when preachers condemned the popular theatre, and was apparently unaware of *2 Henry IV,* which must have been one of the theatrical sensations of 1596–98, suggests that Meres was not up-to-date in theatre affairs in 1598. As a young man he may have been an enthusiast, and certainly he is informed about drama in the earlier nineties: where plays of *c.* 1597–98 are concerned, however, his 'negative testimony' cannot be regarded as significant.

And there is another good reason for distrusting Meres' list. As in other parts of *Palladis Tamia,* where he balances so many of one against so many of another, he cites six comedies and six tragedies. Shakespeare, inconveniently, had completed more comedies than tragedies by 1598, so Meres could only scrape up a total of six tragedies by adding several histories, including *Henry IV.* Yet the plays of *c.* 1597–98 whose dates are in dispute are all comedies; Meres, therefore, attached as he was to his critical balancing, could not name more comedies since he had run out of tragedies. I conclude again that Meres' silence about a comedy (*As You Like It, Merry Wives, Much Ado*) cannot count as a *terminus a quo.*

Anyone interested in the 'early start'–'late start' debate must pay special attention to Meres. For if Meres' silence persuaded Chambers and others to date some of the plays of 1597–98 later than was necessary, it is possible to push back some of the earliest plays to around 1587 without leaving an awkward gap in the 1590s. Meres' silence, on the other hand, must not be invoked as evidence supporting the 'late start' chronology.

(V) HENSLOWE'S 'NE'

Of all the assumptions that have helped to shape the Shakespeare chronology one of the most potent has concerned Henslowe's 'ne', the mysterious letters placed in his Diary against sums received for the performance of certain plays. Only one Shakespearian play was marked 'ne' (*Titus Andronicus*, 23 January 1594), but there are so many links between late Elizabethan plays that the date of one usually has implications for the dating of others, and the dozens of 'ne' entries in Henslowe's Diary have exerted pressure, barely visible and thus all the more effective, against the 'early start' chronology. For 'ne', it has been assumed, must mean 'new' in one sense or another. As Chambers said –

> Henslowe's 'ne', whatever its precise significance, is certainly a mark attached to a play 'the fyrst tyme yt wasse playde.' Generally it seems to have been a new play in the full sense. It is probable that it was sometimes a revised play, and possible that it was sometimes an old play, given by a particular company for the first time. But there is no clear case of this last type, and there are several clear cases in which such a performance was not marked 'ne'.[16]

As it happens, a new version of Henslowe's Diary edited by R. A. Foakes and R. T. Rickert (1961) gives much fuller extracts from Henslowe's pawn accounts than were printed by Greg, and we read in these that many unfortunates took new clothes, etc., to the money-lender. Invariably he entered these as 'new(e)', never as 'ne' – so that the Diary as now published has several dozen 'new(e)' spellings but not a single 'ne' other than the well-known occurrence of 'ne' against payments for plays. Since Henslowe often had room for more letters than 'ne' this consistent variation strongly suggests that 'ne' was not intended to stand for the word 'new', and that Chambers went too far towards identifying 'ne' as 'new' in claiming that a play marked 'ne' seems generally 'to have been a new play in the full sense.' Occasionally, we know, 'ne' signified 'the first time it was played', but, as Chambers' reservations indicate, quite often 'ne' meant something else – and we have no means of knowing what, or how often. In the event, those who take 'ne' as generally referring to a new play in the full sense run the risk of post-dating this play, and all other plays connected with it.

(VI) POST-DATING

E. K. Chambers' tendency to post-date Elizabethan plays was suspected from the first, and was demonstrated by later research – including his own. It is of course perfectly understandable, since a play's *terminus ante quem* (publication, entry in the Stationers' Register, reference to the play in datable documents) will often appear to be more chronologically decisive than its *terminus a quo* (e.g. the date of the play's source, or of literary works or events irrefutably alluded to in the play). Chambers, however, failed to recognise that whereas a *terminus ante quem* is usually a 'hard' date, one that cannot be disputed, the *terminus a quo* may be 'soft' (e.g. the silence of Meres, the absence of allusions to Shakespeare's plays before 1592): in the upshot he gravitated too readily towards the later date.

Three examples will suffice. (a) Chambers, after reading Peter Alexander on Greene and *Henry VI*, found himself obliged to push back the date of *Henry VI* two years (see (i), above). (b) Having discovered Philip Gawdy's letter of 16 November 1587, about an accident at the performance of a play, almost certainly Part 2 of *Tamburlaine*, Chambers realised in 1930 that the two parts of *Tamburlaine* were probably earlier than he had dated them in *The Elizabethan Stage*; and the earlier date is now generally accepted[17]. (c) Chambers in 1930 assigned *Othello* to the year 1604. Then Alfred Hart showed in 1935 that the 'bad' quarto of *Hamlet* (1603) appears to echo *Othello,* and the new Cambridge editors therefore concluded that *Othello* 'can hardly be later than early 1603, and may even belong to 1602'[18].

(VII) 'THE TROUBLESOME RAIGNE'

Chambers made controversial decisions in five of the six cases examined above. (i) While working on *The Elizabethan Stage* he regarded *TR, A Shrew, Contention* and *True Tragedie* as Shakespearian 'source-plays', and this influenced his chronology; in *William Shakespeare* he repudiated *Contention* and *True Tragedie* as 'source-plays', without revising his chronology. (ii) He followed Malone in assuming that Marlowe was one of Shakespeare's predecessors, and that Shakespeare was 'only just taking rank as a dramatist' in 1592. (iii) He was unaware that Meres was such a poor witness. (iv) He assumed that Henslowe's 'ne' generally meant 'new'. (v) No one has accused Chambers of ante-dating plays, but it is as good as certain that he post-dated several.

It will be observed that in each case Chambers made decisions that shore up the 'late start' chronology, and that in each case later research produced new evidence that points the other way. No wonder that F. P. Wilson refused to follow him, and stated instead that 'the chronology of Shakespeare's earliest plays is so uncertain that it has no right to harden into an orthodoxy.' That was in 1951. Shortly thereafter, in 1954, the debate about *King John* and *TR* recommenced, and, as I have suggested, the traditional view (that *TR* preceded *King John*) has survived partly because misunderstandings were not challenged. Having commented on the more important misunderstandings, I shall now return to *TR* – a text that may well turn out to be the key-stone of the early Shakespeare chronology. I want to look more closely at this play, and at its relationship with *King John,* setting aside all preconceptions about an early or late start. My initial assumption will be F. P. Wilson's uncontroversial conclusion, that the early Shakespeare chronology is 'uncertain.'

Two discussions of *TR,* though partly invalidated by later research, remain indispensable. H. Dugdale Sykes[19] argued in 1919 that George Peele wrote *TR*, his evidence being parallel passages and the frequent occurrence of Peele's favourite words and phrases. Rupert Taylor[20], who listed the parallels between *TR* and Marlowe and anonymous plays of the same period, entirely changed our perspectives, however, for the likeliest explanation of all the known parallels is that *TR* is the work of an unknown writer with a memory-box filled with scraps from other men's plays. Here are a few samples from the scores of echoes printed by Dugdale Sykes and Taylor.

(1) '*in stole of dismall hue* / Assist a sillie Nymphe to wayle her woe' (Peele, *Arraignment,* 611); 'And clad this Land *in stole of dismall hieu*' (*TR* 4). (2) 'Then had not *I poore I* bin unhappie' (*Arraignment,* 657); 'Was ever any so infortunate / ... As *I, poore I*' (2 *TR* 843). (3) '*unrip* not so your *shames*' (*Arraignment,* 346); '*unrippe the shamefull* slaunder' (*TR* 87). (4) 'This traitor king hales to their *longest home*' (Peele, *Alcazar,* 25); 'Were he dispatcht unto his *longest home*' (2 *TR* 144). (5) 'No word shall passe *the office of my tong*' (*Alcazar,* 454); 'My heart controules *the office of my toong*' (2 *TR* 23). (6) 'Whose *tongue is tun'd to tell his latest tale*' (Kyd, *Spanish Tragedy,* IV. 4. 85); 'My *tongue is tunde* to storie forth mishap: / When did I breath *to tell* a pleasing *tale*?' (*TR* 1158–9). (7) 'And death arrests *the organe of my voice*' (Marlowe, *Tamburlaine,* II. 7. 8); 'Her passions stop *the organ of her voyce*' (*TR* 1154). (8) 'Thou *proud disturber of thy countries peace*' (*Edward II,* II. 5. 9); '*Proud,* and *disturber of thy Countreyes peace*' (*TR* 1059). (9) 'And *leaue* your grace, and *cleaue* to *Selimus*' (Greene, *Selimus,* 128); 'Will *leave* the French, and *cleave* unto your King' (2 *TR* 691)

Not all the echoes are equally arresting; some are merely unusual turns of phrase, less significant in themselves than in combination with all the others. The cumulative evidence becomes really interesting, however, when we add the parallels with Shakespeare, some of which are known and some of which are now printed for the first time. I begin with two plays where such parallels are particularly common, *3 Henry vi* and *Richard iii*, and then cite others from Shakespeare's early plays.

(1) 'Sham'st thou not, *knowing whence thou art extraught*' (*3 H6*, ii. 2. 142); 'And when thou *knowest from whence thou art extraught*' *(TR* 394). (2) 'Why should she live *to fill the world with words?*'(*3 H6*, v. 5. 44); 'And *fill the world with brawles and mutinies*' (*TR* 742). (3) 'Thy brother's *blood* the *thirsty earth* hath drunk' (*3 H6*, ii. 3. 15); '*bloud . . .* Closing the cranies of the *thirstie earth*' (*TR* 891). (4) 'Now Montague, *sit fast; I seek for thee*' (*3 H6*, v. 2. 3); 'Then Duke *sit fast, I levell at thy head*' (*TR* 924). (5) '*Ah, who is nigh?* Come to me, friend or foe . . . *My mangled body* shows . . . That I must yield my body to the earth' (*3 H6*, v. 2. 5ff.); '*Hoe, who is nigh?* some bodie take me up . . . O God *my bones are burst . . . My vital powers forsake *my brused trunk*' (*2 TR* 12ff.). (6) 'That *from his loins* no hopeful *branch* may *spring*' (*3 H6*, iii. 2. 126); '*From out these loynes* shall *spring* a Kingly braunch' (*2 TR* 1084).

(1) 'Faith, some certain dregs of *conscience* are yet within me . . . What we will do, we do upon *command. – And he that hath commanded is our king. –* Erroneous vassals! the great King of kings / Hath in the tables of his law commanded / That thou shalt do no murder' (*R3*, i. 4. 121, 189ff.); 'I faint, I feare, my *conscience* bids desist . . . *My King commaunds*, that warrants sets me free: / *But God forbids, and he commaundeth Kings*' (*TR* 1433 ff.). (2) 'Now, princely Buckingham, seal thou this *league* . . . A pleasing cordial, princely Buckingham, / Is this thy vow unto my sickly heart. / *There wanteth* now our brother Gloucester here / To make the blessed period of this peace. – / *And, in good time, / Here comes* Sir Richard Ratcliff and the Duke' (*R3*, ii. 1. 29ff.); 'Thrice welcome to the *league* of high resolve . . . *Now wanteth* but the rest to end this worke . . . *And in good time heere come* the warmen all' (*2 TR* 364ff.). (3) '*By a divine instinct* men's minds mistrust' (*R3*, ii. 3. 42); '*By some devine instinct* layd armes aside' (*2 TR* 518). (4) '*Set down, set down* your honourable *load*' (*R3*, i. 2. 1.); '*Set downe, set downe* the *load* not worth your pain' (*2 TR* 786). (5) 'Alas, I rather *hate myself* . . . And, if I die, *no soul will pity me*' (*R3*, v. 3. 189ff.); 'I live and *loath my selfe. / Who pities me*? to whom have I been kinde?' (*2 TR* 790).

It will be noticed that the author of *TR* sometimes appears to recollect a series of phrases from the same scene: (4) and (5) from *3 Henry vi* belong together, and (1) and (2) from *Richard iii* each contain several echoes. In addition, some closely adjacent passages in *TR* repeat phrases that are far apart in Shakespeare ((4) and (5) from *Richard iii*). It seems that certain scenes made a special impression on him, and that when he was in an 'echoing' mood one echo often brought on another.

Next, a selection of echoes from other early Shakespeare plays that left fewer traces in *TR*. (1) 'Even now I curse the *day* ... Wherein I did not *some notorious ill*' (*Titus Andronicus*, v. 1. 125); 'when, and where, have I bestowd a *day* / That tended not to *some notorious ill*?' (*2 TR* 1060).   (2) 'Nay, then 'tis time to stir him from his *trance*. / I pray, *awake*, sir' (*The Shrew*, I. 1. 172); 'Yong man how now, what, art thou in a *traunce*? – *Philip awake*, the man is in a *dreame*' (*TR* 239).   (3) '*Hopeless* and *helpless* doth Aegeon wend' (*Errors*, I. 1. 158); 'Poore *helpless* boy, *hopeles and helples* too' (*TR* 894).   (4) 'Lord Card'nal, if thou think'st on heaven's bliss, / *Hold up thy hand* ... He dies, and makes no sign' (*2 H6*, III. 3. 27); 'in token of thy faith, / And signe thou dyest the servant of the Lord, / *Lift up thy hand*' (*2 TR* 1124).

Are we to suppose that Peele, Marlowe, Shakespeare and others all pilfered phrases and ideas from *TR*, a play strangely uncelebrated by its contemporaries if its impact was so wide-spread? Such an hypothesis is inherently unlikely, and is not helped by the fact that Peele's *Arraignment* was published in 1584. No: all the signs suggest that the author of *TR* was the debtor. His literary talent may be described as essentially derivative, or parasitic: he attempted blank verse, rhymed pentameters, fourteeners, Skeltonics and other forms of doggerel, as well as prose. He was an imitator of popular styles, as well as phrases, and this makes it all the more likely that he also imitated another man's plot.

We must now briefly examine the verbal echoes that link *King John* and *TR*. Here are some examples.   (1) 'To *Ireland, Poyctiers, Aniowe, Torayne, Maine*' (*KJ* I. 1. 11, Folio text); 'with the Lordship of *Ireland, Poiters, Aniow, Torain, Main*', '*Ireland, Poiters, Aniow, Torain, Main*' (*TR* 33, 36). [Bullough (IV. 73) prints '*Poitiers*' in 1. 33 in error (for '*Poiters*'). In this paragraph I cite *TR* from the original, not from Bullough.].   (2) 'Then do I giue *Volquessen, Toraine, Maine*, / *Poyctiers*, and *Aniow*, these fiue Prouinces' (*KJ* II. 1. 527–8, Folio); 'Then I demaund *Volquesson, Torain, Main*, / *Poiters* and *Aniou*, these fiue Prouinces' (*TR* 827–8).   (3) 'All Kent hath yielded; nothing there holds out / But Dover Castle' (*KJ* v. 1. 30–31); 'all places yeeld: / The Land is theirs, and not a foote holds out / But *Douer* Castle' (*2 TR* 644–6).   (4) Melun warns the barons of Lewis' treachery 'For that my grandsire was an Englishman' (v. 4. 42); 'For that my Grandsire was an Englishman' (*2 TR* 748). These, surprisingly, are the closest echoes in the two plays. How are we to explain them? If we think that they look like 'documentary links' (cf. p. 60), because the two plays had a special relationship and one, in these passages, seems to have copied the other, then we must ponder the fact that in (1) and (2), where the two plays happen to repeat Holinshed almost verbatim, it is *King John*,

not *TR*, that is closer to Holinshed's spelling. Both (1) and (2) draw upon
Holinshed's report that when the English and French kings met, the
French king demanded 'the whole countrie of Veulquessine to be restored
vnto him ... Moreouer, he demanded, that Poictiers, Aniou, Maine, and
Touraine, should be deliuered ... vnto Arthur' (p. 160). Since
Shakespeare followed Holinshed in the spelling of *Poyctiers* (and in giving
a final 'e' to Torain*e* and Main*e*), there seems to be a 'documentary link'
between Holinshed and *King John,* so a second 'documentary link' at the
same point (the printed version of *TR* influencing *King John*) must be
regarded with caution. That being so, let us consider the alternative – a
'memorial link', the possibility that one of the two dramatists recalled
these verbal scraps from the other play. The significant thing, in my
opinion, is that the *King John – TR* parallels resemble *TR*'s echoes from
other plays, consisting of lines and phrases of undistinguished verse that
no normal 'imitator' would have picked out. Whereas it was once said
that *TR*, if a derivative play or piracy, should have echoed *King John*
much more closely that it does – an assumption that, I have suggested (p.
57), we are not entitled to make – we may say, instead, that the verbal
'links' between *King John* and *TR* fit in with our general picture of the
TR author – a man suffering from a Pistol syndrome, the irresistible habit
of regurgitating scraps from other men's plays. Even when he was not
aiming to reproduce Shakespeare's dialogue, but saw himself as the writer
of his own King John play, he cannot help echoing his predecessor.

One echo that links *Richard III* and *TR,* which has not received the
attention it deserves, must now be scrutinised more closely. This is no.
(3) on p. 80 where, as A. S. Caincross observed, Shakespeare's immediate
source was Holinshed.

> before such great things, mens hearts of a secret instinct of nature
> misgiue them; as the sea without wind swelleth of himselfe sometime
> before a tempest ...

> Truly, the hearts of men are full of fear .... '
> Before the days of change, still is it so;
> By a divine instinct men's minds mistrust
> Ensuing danger; as by proof we see
> The water swell before a boistrous storm.[21]

Shakespeare's 'By a divine instinct' clearly picked up Holinshed's 'of a
secret instinct of nature'. How then explain 'By some devine instinct' in
TR? It could be argued that, since there are other *Richard III – TR* echoes,
Holinshed's phrase reminded Shakespeare of a phrase from *TR*. This,

however, is to clutch at straws; only the fixed idea that *TR* is pre-Shakespearian will drive us to such a conclusion. If we keep an open mind about the chronology of Shakespeare's first plays, and do not lose sight of the fact that phrases and lines in *TR* so strangely resemble others in so many contemporary plays, the obvious explanation is that Shakespeare coined the phrase 'By a divine instinct' after reading Holinshed, and that the author of *TR* once again pilfered from a play. It cannot be claimed as certain but, all things considered, it seems very much more likely than the alternative.

We are now ready to return to *TR* and *King John*. I want to look first at two curious and related points. (1) *TR* (like *A Shrew*) was first identified as one of Shakespeare's sources when the 'bad quarto' texts of six plays (*Romeo, Henry V, Merry Wives, Hamlet, 2 + 3 Henry VI*) were all thought to be sources as well. Now that the six texts (and also *A Shrew*[22]) are explained differently, we have to ask whether the traditional view of *TR*, as the 'source' of *King John*, is a hang-over from an outmoded theory. For *TR* is much closer to *King John* than any other surviving source-play to Shakespeare's re-working, being mostly followed scene by scene, and sometimes speech by speech, in *King John*. Indeed, it must be stressed that Shakespeare's dependence upon this 'source-play' is unique, if source it is.

(2) The unknown author of *TR* had little or no poetic talent. He was capable of writing speeches that are little better than verse gabble, and he appears to have tried to compensate for his deficiencies by imitating his more expert contemporaries. As far as we know, he wrote no other play. Is it likely that this man could have devised a plot that satisfied Shakespeare more completely than any other that he borrowed from a predecessor?

In both cases there is an anomaly that involves the play's plotting. It is strange that Shakespeare, usually so high-handed in his rearrangement of source-material, departed from his normal practice in *King John* – if *King John* followed *TR*; and it is equally strange that the plotting of *TR* is so much more professional than this otherwise unknown author's minimal literary talent would lead us to expect. Both anomalies vanish if *TR* is regarded as a derivative play, based on *King John*.

Now let us ponder a third and equally curious anomaly. It has long been known that eighteen hitherto unpublished plays first appeared in the Folio, but that only sixteen of the eighteen were entered in the Stationers' Register in 1623. The two that were omitted were *The Taming of the Shrew* and *King John*. These two plays, thought E. K. Chambers, 'must have been allowed to pass as reprints of the old plays, *The Taming of A*

Shrew and *The Troublesome Reign of John'* – an explanation also accepted by Greg[23]. No one has cited an instance of a play or book 'allowed to pass' merely because it dealt with the same story as an earlier work; and it would have been an odd principle for the stationers to apply – it would have lost them a lot of fees, and would have led to endless confusion about who owned which 'copy'. On the other hand, 'bad quarto' texts were normally and frequently treated as identical with the 'good' version as far as 'copyright' was concerned. The most natural explanation of the fact that no SR entry was deemed necessary for *The Shrew* and *King John* in 1623 must be that *Shakespeare's colleagues considered A Shrew and TR to be 'bad quartos' which had already established 'copy-right'.* Now that expert opinion is moving more and more towards acceptance of *A Shrew* as a 'bad quarto'[24] we can see that Heminge and Condell's failure to have *King John* entered in the SR becomes even more significant. They were aware of the existence of 'stolne, and surreptitious copies, maimed, and deformed by the frauds and stealthes of iniurious impostors', and appear to have thought that *A Shrew,* though more deformed than others, was also 'stolne, and surreptitious.' That leaves *King John* as the lonely exception, the one play for which we have to invent the improbable theory that a source-play (*TR*) established its copyright. Is it not more likely that in this instance, again, Heminge and Condell knew what they were doing, and that the decision not to enter *King John* in the SR argues powerfully for the view that *TR* was also 'stolne and surreptitious'?

The fact that *TR* contains so many unusual tags and phrases, almost certainly echoes from Peele, Marlowe, Shakespeare and others, points to a similar conclusion – that the author of *TR* was a shameless borrower. Why, then, are there still traditionalists who refuse to accept that *TR* could have borrowed from *King John*? Partly because it is assumed that the author of *TR,* if this play came after *King John,* would have wanted to reproduce Shakespeare's dialogue exactly – which, as I have argued, does not follow (p. 57); and partly because these traditionalists are imprisoned in the 'late start' chronology and think that it prohibits a date as early as 1590–91 for *King John.* But their prison walls fell down long ago, and they are more free than they imagine: to repeat again F. P. Wilson's words, 'the chronology of Shakespeare's earliest plays is so uncertain that it has no right to harden into an orthodoxy'[25]. The 'late start' chronology, as I have tried to show in more detail, is a tissue of assumptions, inherited by E. K. Chambers from his predecessors, most of which have been seriously questioned or disproved by later research.

One other explanation of *TR* still needs to be considered. E. M. W. Tillyard agreed with Peter Alexander that 'as an authentic, consistent, and self-supporting composition the *Troublesome Reign* cannot pass. The masterly construction is quite at odds with the heterogeneous execution'[26]; nevertheless, Tillyard would not accept *TR* as a bad quarto of *King John* and proposed a third possibility – that there could have been a third King John play, a lost early version by Shakespeare (let us call it *Lost KJ*), which was pirated by the author of *TR* and later revised by Shakespeare as *King John*. One of Tillyard's reasons for hypothesising a *Lost KJ* in 1944 must have been the wish to bring Alexander's disturbing new ideas about *TR* safely under the umbrella of the 'late start' chronology. But was it really necessary to postulate a lost play? One new fact brought to light since 1944, Cairncross's discovery that *TR* almost certainly echoes a passage from *Richard III* where *Richard III* echoes Holinshed (see p. 82), has important consequences. If we accept that *TR* was written after *Richard III*, we have to ask whether the stylistic or metrical evidence compels us to date *King John* much later than *Richard III*, or whether the two plays could reasonably be assigned to the same year or two – in which case both *Richard III* and *King John* could have preceded *TR*. While E. K. Chambers placed *King John* four years after *Richard III*, his metrical tables cannot be said to support a four-year gap, nor, indeed, to prove that the two plays were written in the same year or two: the tables indicate that both plays were early, and little more. It is worth recalling that the order of the early comedies remains by general consent 'uncertain'[27], and that the order of all the early plays is much more speculative than that of Shakespeare's later work.

Once it is realised that there is no compelling reason for regarding *King John* as more mature than *Richard III*, the need for postulating *Lost KJ* disappears. *Richard III* can hardly be later than 1590–91, being echoed by *TR*; if *Richard III* and *King John* need not be separated by four years, the simplest explanation of *TR* would be that it followed hard upon the success of *King John*, and was the work of an actor (or possibly of an enthusiastic theatre-goer) who recollected lines and phrases from *Richard III* and from *3 Henry VI* and other popular plays, as he threw together his parasitic version of *King John*. I say threw together because, although the author of *TR* certainly read the chronicles, he also wrote in great haste. His mingle-mangle style gives him away –

> Let not these eares receive the hissing sound
> Of such a viper, who with poysoned words
> Doth masserate the bowels of my soule. (140–42)
> This grose attaint so tilteth in my thoughts,
> Maintaining combat to abridge my ease, (329–30)

We must obscure this mone with melodie (902)
Deepe sorrow throbbeth misbefalne events (1155)

Self-repetition is another feature of the text. Words and phrases appear to
be echoed unconsciously –

Who *tempred terror* with his wanton talke (399)
Let shadowe *temper terror* in his thoughts (662)

– and the like, exactly as *TR* appears to echo other texts. And, significantly, such self-repetition sometimes picks up phrases from other
writers as well –

I beg some instance *whence I am extraught* (341)
And when thou *knowest from whence thou art extraught* (394)
On strong instinct hath framd this conventickle (*2 TR* 382)
By some devine instinct layd armes aside (*2 TR* 518)

(compare 'Sham'st thou not, *knowing whence thou art extraught*', 'By a
divine instinct men's minds mistrust', discussed above, pp. 80, 82).
Whether the author of *TR* echoes himself or pilfers from others, we
observe the same procedure: too often he snatches at the first phrase that
occurs to him, and thus achieves the strange patch-work effect that is so
characteristic of his verse.

   If, as I have suggested, *TR* was not written till 1590–91, how is it that
it also came to be printed in 1591? Would that not involve an abnormally
short interval between first production and publication? Yes, it would;
but the Queen's Men, the owners of the play, were having a rough time
in 1591, and unusual conditions explain unusual actions. The 'most
famous of all the London companies during the decade of the eighties',
the Queen's Men had lost several of their best actors by 1590, including
Tarlton and Knell[28]. They performed at Court five times in the Christmas
season of 1590–91, but were already splitting into two troupes, one of
which also played together with Sussex's Men. There are other signs that
they were well on the way to the disaster recorded by Henslowe in 1593,
'to the Quenes players when they brocke & went into the contrey to
playe'[29]: they were only invited to perform once at Court during the
Christmas season of 1591–92 (Strange's Men were called six times); and,
thought Chambers, it was probably in 1591 'that Greene, having sold
Orlando Furioso to the Queen's men for twenty nobles, resold it "when
they were in the country" to the Admiral's for as much more'; as Greg

showed, however, it is more likely that the Queen's Men themselves sold *Orlando* to the Admiral's, because they were desperately short of money, then reconstructed the play from memory and continued to perform it[30]. Chambers added that

> it may fairly be reckoned as another sign of defeat that while *The Troublesome Reign of King John* (1591) was the only play certainly theirs which was printed before 1594, no less than nine found their way into the publishers' hands during that and the following year.

The financial difficulties of the Queen's Men explain why the company might pass on a fairly new play such as *TR* to a printer. But the events that I have just summarised also help to solve a greater mystery: how did the author of *TR* hit upon the idea of writing a reconstructed version of *King John* in the first place? He must have been one of the very earliest to attempt theatrical piracy at this time. If he was connected with the Queen's Men, who, as Greg has shown, at about this time[31] reconstructed one of their own plays after selling it to another company and went on performing it, why not reconstruct another company's get-penny and perform it as well? The Queen's Men were in trouble, and willing to take risks. Suppose they were unable to effect a word-by-word reconstruction, it would make sense to adapt a story that had caught the public's imagination and to expand whatever had seemed most popular (the part of Faulconbridge, by adding the friar-scenes; anti-Catholic speeches and scenes). Had *TR* belonged to another company, in more settled times, the suggestion that it was a stolen and surreptitious copy by an injurious impostor might seem hard to swallow. The special circumstances of the Queen's Men in 1591 are, however, an integral part of our story, and of the case against *TR*[32].

It will be clear by now that I consider the case against *TR* a strong one. That is not, at present, the general view. I have stated it at some length because recent participators in the debate have concentrated on one approach or another, and have not always looked at the wider implications. These include the Shakespeare chronology, and the uncertainty of the dates of his first plays; a tissue of echoes in *TR* from earlier plays; Shakespeare's quite exceptional failure to re-arrange the plotting of his source-play, if *TR* was a source-play; the anomalous treatment of the 'copy-right' for *King John* in 1623, which ceases to be anomalous if *TR* was a stolen and surreptitious copy; the special difficulties of the Queen's Men in 1591, and the likelihood that they were involved in the 'reconstruction' of plays at this very time. In addition, defenders of *TR* as a source-play have employed arguments that work both ways, or have over-looked relevant facts. It would be presumptuous to claim that the case against *TR* as a Shakespearian source-play has now been proved beyond all doubt; I do claim, though, that the traditional view of *TR*, inherited from the eighteenth century, deserves our healthy scepticism. Both explanations of *TR* leave some questions unanswered; but, as I have tried to show, the really difficult questions vanish once we accept that *TR* could have followed *King John*.

(VIII) THE DATES OF SHAKESPEARE'S FIRST PLAYS

What, now, can be said for the 'early start' chronology, and how does it fit in with the other surviving evidence about Shakespeare in the 1580s? Let us begin with the possibility (I think it a probability) that *King John* preceded *TR*, and let us remember that four other plays can reasonably be assigned 'early start' dates. The five dates that emerge (*Titus Andronicus, c.* 1584–89; *Richard III*, 1590–91; *King John*, 1590–91; *Romeo and Juliet*, 1591; *Love's Labour's Lost*, 1592)[33] are based on different kinds of external evidence, and are not contradicted as a sequence by the internal evidence of Shakespeare's stylistic development. Keeping in mind that in the early histories Shakespeare was indebted to the second edition of Holinshed's *Chronicles* (1587), we arrived at a general chronology for the first plays that may be outlined roughly as follows: 1586, *Titus Andronicus*; 1587, *Two Gentlemen of Verona*; 1588, *1 Henry VI, Taming of the Shrew*; 1589, *2 Henry VI, Comedy of Errors*; 1590, *3 Henry VI, Richard III*; 1591, *King John, Romeo and Juliet*; 1592, *Love's Labour's Lost*. These dates are not meant to be definitive: some may be a year or two out. (The order of the first three comedies is, as everyone agrees, uncertain, and *1 Henry VI* could have been written after *3 Henry VI*). I merely wish to indicate that, taking the five more or less 'fixed' dates as starting-points we can arrange around them the other early plays that are usually thought their contemporaries, without arm-twisting any 'fixed' chronological evidence to the contrary.

As is well known, the plague broke out in London in August, 1592, and was particularly severe throughout 1593. Plays were prohibited on 28 January 1593, and regular performances did not recommence until the spring of 1594. At this time, when a career in the theatre must have seemed a risky prospect, Shakespeare turned his talents to the writing of *Venus and Adonis* (SR, 18 April 1593) and *The Rape of Lucrece* (SR, 9 May 1594). The plague years are therefore a convenient terminus for Shakespeare's first plays, or 'first period.' He was deflected into a new kind of writing, and may have stopped writing plays altogether for a year or so. Let us stop at this point as well, and take account of the other facts and probabilities in the story. Shakespeare's marriage to Anne Hathaway (November 1582), the christening of the first child, Susanna (May 1583), and of the twins, Hamnet and Judith (February 1585): these are the bare facts, but we can add several plausible appendices. First, that 'He understood Latine pretty well: for he had been in his younger yeares a Schoolmaster in the Countrey' (John Aubrey's note, from William Beeston[34]); second, that he probably left school *c.* 1580, without proceeding to a university. Though Aubrey's 'School-master' probably meant assistant teacher rather than master-in-charge, or possibly private teacher in a well-to-do household, such a post would scarcely be offered to one who had himself left school at the earliest opportunity and had taken no degree: whence I conjecture that the future dramatist remained at school till *c.* 1580.

Apart from the school-master story, which comes to us from an excellent source, we must consider another snippet of information about Shakespeare's career from *c.* 1580 to 1592. In Rowe's *Life* of Shakespeare (1709), which was partly based on anecdotes supplied by Thomas Betterton, the actor, who had made a special journey to Stratford to glean whatever local gossip he could, we read –

> His Father, who was a considerable Dealer in Wool, had so large a Family, ten Children in all, that tho' he was his eldest Son, he could give him no better Education than his own Employment. He had bred him, 'tis true, for some time at a Free-School . . . [35]

Since it is certain, from Stratford records, that Shakespeare's father was a glover, Rowe's story appears to be contradicted by a better authority. Nevertheless, it was reported early in the nineteenth century that when the floors of the parlour of John Shakespeare's house were taken up, 'the remnants of wool, and the refuse of wool-combing, were found under the old flooring, imbedded with the earth of the foundation'; and, more recently, Leslie Hotson has discovered that in 1599 John Shakespeare sued John Walford, a clothier who was three times Mayor of Marlborough in Wiltshire, 'on a debt of £21; alleging that on November 4, 1568, at Stratford-on-Avon, Walford bought twenty-one tods of wool of him for £21'[36]. Evidently John Shakespeare was a glover and also 'a considerable Dealer in Wool'. (The school-master at the King's School, Stratford, was given a house rent-free, and a salary of £20 p.a., so £21 was a 'considerable' sum). The truth of Rowe's story has been vindicated; we must therefore take Rowe's conclusion seriously – that John Shakespeare could give his son 'no better Education that his own Employment'. This suggests that William worked for a while with his father, an inherently probable arrangement since he was the eldest son.

Still another conjecture about Shakespeare's activities from 1580 to 1592 must be considered. It is widely believed that he joined a company of actors, and earned his living as a performer before commencing as a dramatist. Whether or not Greene meant that the 'vpstart Crow' was an actor turned dramatist, or Chettle referred to acting in acknowledging Shakespeare 'exelent in the qualitie he professes' – I think both interpretations disputable[37] – there are enough later allusions to Shakespeare as an actor to make it plausible that he began his theatrical career by joining a company of actors. Since Shakespeare was to stay in the theatre, it looks as if his school-mastering and his stint in his father's business came first; both of these early careers could have been completed, however, by 1585, when the twins were born. The other available facts about Shakespeare in the 1580s, and Aubrey's and Rowe's two anecdotes, our only additional information of any value, leave us free to date Shakespeare's first play *c.* 1586 and in no sense contradict the 'early start' chronology. On the other hand, as I have mentioned, Greene's sense of Shakespeare's unique position ('in his owne conceit the onely Shake-scene in a countrey') confirms that by 1592 Shakescene's pre-eminence rested on something more than just three or four plays.

Moving back Shakespeare's first play from 1590 to *c.* 1586, we make his commencement as a dramatist contemporary with that of his exact coeval, Christopher Marlowe. Instead of seeing Shakespeare as a follower of the University Wits, arriving on the literary scene when the new drama had already been set on its course by Lyly, Peele, Kyd, Marlowe, Greene etc., we can assume that Shakespeare's impact helped significantly at an earlier stage. But the case for an 'early start' chronology, it must be repeated, depends appreciably, though not exclusively, on the argument that *TR* is a derivative play. Those who consider the traditional 'late start' chronology sacrosanct will, of course, brush away this view of *TR* as quirky and 'way out.' I have suggested that the traditional Malone–Chambers chronology is far from sacrosanct, and that an early date for *King John* must not be seen as an isolated challenge to a fixed chronology but rather as an integral part of a coherent, alternative chronology. This is not the place to re-scrutinise the internal and external evidence for all of Shakespeare's early plays in the minutest detail. If I am right about *King John* and *TR*, however, Shakespeare's early impact as a contemporary of the University Wits will have to be reassessed, and the dramatic history of the late Elizabethan age will have to be re-written.

5
Contemporary Criticisms of Shakespeare

Amidst all the contemporary praise of Shakespeare, as a poet and dramatist, what more critical attitudes, if any, can we discern? The very first surviving allusion, in Greene's *Groats-Worth of Witte* (*GWW*), remarked unflatteringly that Shake-scene 'supposes he is as well able to bombast out [i.e. to swell out (with bombastic language)] a blanke verse as the best' – a view that cannot be dismissed as purely malicious since it was echoed by others. Dryden reported, presumably from hearsay, that in 'reading some bombast speeches of *Macbeth,* which are not to be understood, he [Jonson] used to say that it was horrour'[1]. Dryden, though he expressed himself more generously elsewhere, shared Greene's and Jonson's attitude when he wrote in his Preface to *Troilus and Cressida* (1679):

> [Shakespeare's] whole style is so pestered with figurative expressions, that it is as affected as it is obscure .... I will not say of so great a poet, that he distinguished not the blown puffy style from true sublimity; but I may venture to maintain, that the fury of his fancy often transported him beyond the bounds of judgment.[2]

Jonson and Dryden, like Greene, had their reasons for being hard on Shakespeare's style; Jonson, committed to a different kind of drama, publicly advocated 'language such as men do use', and Dryden had undertaken to correct *Troilus* and wanted the world to be grateful. Nevertheless, others had mocked Shakespeare's stylistic excesses without any selfish motive, and we must accept, I think, that contemporaries were sometimes less inclined to admire than to smile at his style. (As I have mentioned (p. 37), the plays that were ridiculed were not all available in print until 1623, which made it difficult to do them justice). In *The Knight of the Burning Pestle* (*KBP*), (*c.* 1607), Ralph the Prentice, called on by the Citizen's Wife to 'speak a huffing part', declaims

91

By heaven, methinks it were an easy leap
To pluck bright honour from the pale-fac'd moon . . . .

While Shakespeare was not necessarily discredited by being praised by the undiscriminating (e.g. Gullio in the *Parnassus* play, quoted p. 15), it is relevant that in *KBP* we are not merely invited to smile at the simplicity of Ralph and Citizen's Wife but, more particularly, at bad writing. Beaumont and Fletcher, soon to be closely associated with the King's Men if not already so, agreed with Greene and Jonson that there was too much 'huffing'[3] in Shakespeare.

Before we pass judgment on such insensitive contemporaries we must refer once more to the historical context. Towards the turn of the century an important argument developed between upholders of different views of language. Sometimes seen merely as a disagreement about 'inkhorn terms', it opened out into a debate about linguistic decorum. Spenser, Marlowe and Shakespeare were key figures because, in different ways, they tried to stretch language and to extend the limits of the permissible – a preoccupation of the 1580s and 1590s reflected in the verbal gambolling of *Love's Labour's Lost*. Opposing this new use of language, Greene complained in *Perimedes* (1588) that he had been derided

> for that I could not make my verses iet vpon the stage in tragicall buskins, everie word filling the mouth like the Faburden of Bo-Bell, daring God out of heaven with that Atheist *Tamburlan* . . . .

The following year Nashe expanded on this, picking on the author of a Senecan tragedy called *Hamlet* as one of the villains –

> the Alcumists of eloquence, who (mounted on the stage of arrogance) thinke to out-braue better pennes with the swelling bumbast of a bragging blanke verse.[4]

Greene's attack on Shake-scene in *GWW* echoed Nashe's very phrasing[5]; Nashe himself, however, also tried 'swelling bumbast' techniques in prose, and even boasted 'I haue tearmes . . . laide in steepe in *Aquafortis, &* Gunpowder, that shall rattle through the Skyes, and make an Earthquake in a Pesants eares'[6].

The newly discovered vigour of the English language created a special problem for writers who believed that tragedy requires a 'high style'. In the induction of Day's *Isle of Gulls* two gentlemen discuss poetry, and one demands 'stately', 'high writ' verse, the other scorns it. The Prologue then explains the dramatist's dilemma:

> If he compose a scene
> Of high writ poesy, fitting a true stage,
> 'Tis counted fustian.

It must have been a familiar debate in and around London's theatres. We hear its reverberations when Jonson publicly praised Marlowe's 'mighty line' while privately noting that the

> true Artificer will not run away from nature, as hee were afraid of her; or depart from life, and the likenesse of Truth ... And though his language differ from the vulgar somewhat; it shall not fly from all humanity, with the *Tamerlanes,* and *Tamer-Chams* of the late Age, which had nothing in them but the *scenicall* strutting, and furious vociferation[7].

Side by side with contemporary praise of Shakespeare's 'mellifluous' style, mindlessly reiterated, and much rarer commendations of a more thoughtful kind[8], we find adverse comments on his style which, placed in their historical context, are the first warning signals that another view of language was possible, and would prevail. Shakespeare's 'high writ poesy' could be counted fustian. Dryden, weighing his greatest predecessors, decided that Shakespeare 'is many times flat, insipid; his comic wit degenerating into clenches, his serious swelling into bombast'; Beaumont and Fletcher, on the other hand, 'understood and imitated the conversation of gentlemen much better ... I am apt to believe the English language in them arrived to its highest perfection'[9].

Leaving aside 'huffing', what other unfavourable comment survives from Shakespeare's contemporaries? More than a little. Oddly, though, it all comes from one man, Ben Jonson, who returned to the attack again and again. Most of Jonson's criticisms are well known, and need not detain us for long; I reprint them in order to throw light on less familiar Shakespeare-Jonson exchanges, including the *Sonnets* and *The Winter's Tale,* and to show that Jonson's remarks, even if sometimes querulous in tone, hang together and make a formidable indictment.

(a) General attacks on the improbability of Shakespeare's plotting

(i) A Prologue written *c.* 1605 for *Every Man In His Humour (EMIH)* lists the 'ill customes' of contemporary drama (*Henry VI* and *Henry V*):

To make a child, now swadled, to proceede
Man, and then shoote vp, in one beard, and weede,
Past threescore yeeres: or, with three rustie swords,
And helpe of some few foot-and-halfe-foote words,
Fight ouer *Yorke,* and *Lancasters* long iarres:
And in the tyring-house bring wounds, to scarres.
He [Jonson] rather prayes, you will be pleas'd to see
One such, to day, as other playes should be.
Where neither *Chorus* wafts you ore the seas;
Nor creaking throne comes downe, the boyes to please; . . .
But deedes, and language, such as men doe vse;
And persons, such as *Comoedie* would chuse,
When she would show an Image of the times, . . .

(ii) The Induction of *Bartholomew Fair* (1614) condemns *The Winter's Tale*
and *The Tempest*:

If there bee neuer a *Seruant-monster* i' the *Fayre;* who can helpe it? he
[Jonson] sayes; nor a nest of *Antiques?* Hee is loth to make Nature
afraid in his *Playes,* like those that beget *Tales, Tempests,* and such like
Drolleries, to mix his head with other mens heeles, let the concupisence
of *Iigges* and *Dances,* raigne as strong as it will amongst you.

(iii) In conversation with William Drummond, 1619, Jonson picked on
another improbability in *The Winter's Tale*:

Sheakespear in a play brought in a number of men saying they had
suffered Shipwrack in Bohemia, wher ther is no Sea by some 100 Miles.

(iv) *Ode to Himselfe,* composed after the failure of *The New Inn* (1629),
ridiculed *Pericles*:

No doubt some mouldy tale,
    Like *Pericles;* and stale
As the Shrieues crusts, and nasty as his fish —
    scraps, out of euery dish,
Throwne forth, and rak't into the common tub,
    May keepe vp the *Play-club*:
There, sweepings doe as well
As the best order'd meale.

Under (*a*) I have grouped criticisms of Shakespeare's disregard of the 'unities' of time and place, and criticisms of the inherited conventions of 'mouldy' romance. Here, of course, Jonson echoed earlier writers, such as Gosson and Sidney, who had already deplored such developments in the 1580s.

> Sometime you shall see nothing but the aduentures of an amorous knight, passing from countrie to countrie for the loue of his lady, encountring many a terible monster made of broune paper, & at his retorne, is so wonderfully changed, that he can not be knowne but by some posie in his tablet, or by a broken ring, or a handkircher, or a piece of a cockle shell. What learne you by that?

> the player, when he cometh in, must ever begin with telling where he is, or else the tale will not be conceived. Now ye shall have three ladies walk to gather flowers and then we must believe the stage to be a garden. By and by we hear news of ship-wreck in the same place, and then we are to blame if we accept it not for a rock ... While in the meantime two armies fly in, represented with four swords and bucklers, and then what hard heart will not receive it for a pitched field?[10]

(b) Ridicule of Shakespeare's too fluent writing, of nonsense passages and of the incorrect use of words

(i) The most explicit attack came after Shakespeare's death, in 'De Shakespeare nostrati' (Appendix A, p. 125). (ii) Before that, Jonson drew attention to words and lines 'which were ridiculous'. For example, two passages in *Julius Caesar*.

> O judgment, thou art fled to brutish beasts
> And men have lost their reason! (III. 2. 104–5)

Compare *EMOH* III. 4. 33: '*Reason long since is fled to animals,* you know'. A second passage which, if we may believe Jonson, originally read 'Caesar did never wrong, but with just cause' (cf. *JC* III. 1. 47–8), was cited in 'De Shakespeare nostrati' (cf. below, p. 126), and again in the induction of *The Staple of News* (1626), '*Cry you mercy,* you neuer did wrong, but with iust cause'. (iii) In *Poetaster* (1601) Jonson mocked the dramatists who opposed him in the War of the Theatres. Crispinus (Marston) is given an emetic and is made to bring up new words coined by him that displeased Jonson; among these are words not used by Marston, but found in Shakespeare, another opponent of Jonson in the War: retrograde and defunct (*Poet.* v. 3. 275, 278; cf. *Hamlet*, i. 2. 114; 'It is most retrograde to our desire'; *Henry v*, iv. 1. 21). (iv) In the *EMIH* Prologue (cited above (a)(i), p. 94), it is all too clear that Shakespeare has sinned against 'language, such as men doe vse'.

(c) Jonson's 'Discoveries'

We now come to Jonson's paragraph 'De Shakespeare nostrati' which, perhaps more than any of his other comments, needs to be considered in its immediate context, as part of a much larger passage – a point left unexplained by biographers and by the *Shakspere Allusion-Book*. The paragraph occurs in Jonson's *Discoveries*, a series of seemingly disjointed notes, many of them translations from classical authors, some of which pursue related ideas and hang together as loosely structured essays. The Shakespeare paragraph is the centre-piece of one such essay, and cannot be properly understood if read on its own. A summary of the general drift of thought, with line-references to the Oxford *Ben Jonson* (vol. viii), will be useful.

(i) *De vere Argutis* (Concerning the truly witty; lines 570–86). Jonson complains that 'Nothing is fashionable, till it bee deform'd; and this is to write like a *Gentleman*. All must bee as affected, and preposterous as our Gallants cloathes ...'

(ii) *Censura de Poetis* (Judgment of poets; lines 587–646) (*a*) Nothing 'is more preposterous' than opinions about poetry; 'those men' are 'almost nam'd for *Miracles*' who, 'if a man should goe about, to ... correct them, hee must make all they have done, but one blot. Their good is so intangled with their bad ... Yet their vices have not hurt them ... for they have beene lov'd for nothing else.' (*b*) '*Indeed*, the multitude commend Writers, as they doe Fencers, or Wrastlers; who if they come in robustiously, and put for it, with a deale of violence, are received for the *braver-fellowes*: when many times their owne rudenesse is cause of their disgrace; and a slight touch of their Adversary, gives all that boisterous force the foyle. But in these things, the unskilfull are naturally deceiv'd, and judging wholly by the bulke, thinke rude things greater then polish'd; and scatter'd more numerous, then compos'd.'

(iii) *De Shakespeare nostrati.* (Concerning our fellow Shakespeare; lines 647–68. Reprinted in full in Appendix A, p. 125). The players commended Shakespeare because 'hee never blotted out line'; Jonson replied 'Would he had blotted [deleted] a thousand.' Shakespeare 'flow'd with that facility, that sometime it was necessary he should be stop'd'. Many times 'hee fell into those things, could not escape laughter ... which were ridiculous.'

(iv) *Ingeniorum discrimina* (The differences of wits; lines 669–800). (*a*) 'Some wits are swelling, and high; others low and still ... One must have a bridle, the other a spurre.' (*b*) Some 'presuming on their owne *Naturals* (which perhaps are excellent) dare deride all diligence, and seeme to mock at the termes, when they understand not the things; thinking that way to get off wittily, with their Ignorance ... and the more wilfull, and stubborne, they are in it, the more learned they are esteem'd of the *multitude,* through their excellent vice of Judgement'. (*c*) '*It cannot* but come to passe, that these men, who commonly seeke to doe more then enough, may sometimes happen on some thing that is good, and great; but very seldome: And when it comes, it doth not recompence the rest of their ill. For their jests ... sticke out, and are more eminent; because all is sordid, and vile about them; as lights are more discern'd in a thick darkenesse, then a faint shadow. Now because they speake all they can (how ever unfitly) they are thought to have the greater copy; Where the learned use ever election, and a meane.' (*d*) 'The true Artificer will not run away from nature, as hee were afraid of her; or depart from life, and the likenesse of Truth ... And though his language differ from the vulgar somewhat [,] it shall not fly from all humanity ... Perhaps hee [the true Artificer, i.e. Jonson] is call'd barren, dull, leane, a poore Writer ... by these men, who without labour, judgement, knowledge, or almost sense, are received, or preferr'd before him.'

The argument moves from true and false wit (i) to good and bad poets, and skilful and unskilful judgment of poets (ii). *De Shakespeare nostrati* (iii) illustrates good and bad writing, and skilful and unskilful judgement (Jonson; the players); (iv) returns to true and false wit (*a*), unskilful judgement (*b*), bad writers (*c*), and the aims of the good writer (Jonson, the true artificer) (*d*). Apart from the continuity of Jonson's general thinking, other threads also hold the four passages (i-iv) together. False wit and false judgement are 'preposterous' (i, ii), Shakespeare's bad lines are 'ridiculous'; the work of admired writers, if corrected, would become 'one blot' (ii, *a*), Shakespeare should have 'blotted a thousand'; Shakespeare's wit needed to 'be stop'd', '*Sufflaminandus erat*' (he needed the drag-chain), as swelling wits 'must have a bridle' (iv, *a*). Even if there were no other supporting evidence we would have to conclude that the Shakespeare paragraph knits firmly together with (i), (ii) and (iv); fortunately, though, the internal evidence of the text is supported by external evidence that puts the issue beyond question. For, as is well known, some of the passages that I have quoted repeat verbatim sentences from Jonson's 'To the Reader' prefixed to *The Alchemist* (1612):

TO THE READER.

IF thou beest more, thou art an Vnderstander, and then I trust thee. If thou art one that tak'st vp, and but a Pretender, beware at what hands thou receiu'st thy commoditie; for thou wert neuer more fair in the way to be cos'ned (then in this Age) in Poetry, especially in Playes: wherein, now, the Concupiscence of Daunces, and Antickes so raig-   5
neth, as to runne away from Nature, and be afraid of her, is the onely point of art that tickles the Spectators. But how out of purpose, and place, doe I name Art? when the Professors are growne so obstinate contemners of it, and presumers on their owne Naturalls, as they are deriders of all diligence that way, and, by simple mocking at the   10
termes, when they vnderstand not the things, thinke to get of wittily with their Ignorance. Nay, they are esteem'd the more learned, and sufficient for this, by the Many, through their excellent vice of iudge-ment. For they commend Writers, as they doe Fencers, or Wrastlers; who if they come in robustuously, and put for it with a great deale of   15
violence, are receiu'd for the brauer fellowes: when many times their owne rudenesse is the cause of their disgrace, and a little touch of their Aduersary giues all that boisterous force the foyle. I deny not, but that these men, who alwaies seeke to doe more then inough, may some time happen on some thing that is good, and great; but very seldome: 20
And when it comes it doth not recompencé the rest of their ill. It sticks out perhaps, and is more eminent, because all is sordide, and vile about it: as lights are more discern'd in a thick darknesse, then a faint shadow. I speake not this, out of a hope to doe good on any man, against his will; for I know, if it were put to the question of theirs, and   25
mine, the worse would finde more suffrages: because the most favour common errors. But I giue thee this warning, that there is a great difference between those, that (to gain the opinion of Copie) vtter all they can, how euer vnfitly; and those that vse election, and a meane. For it is onely the disease of the vnskilfull, to thinke rude things   30
greater then polish'd: or scatter'd more numerous then compos'd.

Here we find the sources[11] of (ii, *b*) in 'To the reader' lines 14–18, 30–1; of (iv, *b*) in lines 9–14; of (iv, *c*) in lines 19–24, 28–9; of (iv, *d*) in lines 6, 26. The important point to notice is that Jonson's quarrel with 'these men', all of a piece in 'To the Reader', is echoed *before and after* the Shakespeare paragraph in *Discoveries;* or, to put it differently, is interrupted by the Shakespeare paragraph and then resumed. I deduce that Shakespeare was one of 'these men' – and, since he figures so prominently in *Discoveries,* was seen by Jonson as their leader or as their best example of the poet who writes without 'labour'. This inference is borne out by the fact that in *Discoveries* Jonson echoed not only the *Alchemist* epistle but also other adverse remarks of his own that pointed explicitly at Shakespeare. In the Prologue of *Every Man In His Humour* (quoted above, p. 94) he criticised the author of *Henry VI* and *Henry V,* proposing as his own alternative 'deedes, and language, such as men doe vse' and comedy that is 'an Image of the times'; in the Induction of *Bartholomew Fair* (quoted p. 94) he described himself as 'loth to make Nature afraid', unlike the author of '*Tales, Tempests*' etc. – two attacks repeated in *Discoveries* (4, *d*), except that 'to make Nature afraid' is turned round, the bad writer being 'afraid of her'.

Once we see that *De Shakespeare nostrati* is part of a much longer discussion that centres on Shakespeare we begin to understand something already visible in Jonson's previously identified allusions – a touch of obsessiveness, not unlike his almost manic hatred of Inigo Jones. Except that he did not hate Shakespeare: on the contrary, 'I lov'd the man, and doe honour his memory (on this side Idolatry) as much as any'. Shakespeare, though, was an admired contradiction of all that Jonson stood for, an obstacle to Jonson's proper recognition as dangerous as Inigo Jones and, since it was impossible to hate him, all the more frustrating. In *Discoveries,* written after Shakespeare's death, when Jonson himself was no longer 'the stage's jewel', he meditates bitterly about the decline of his own popularity, inextricably bound up as it is with the general enthusiasm for his rival, and cheers himself with the thought that the multitude cannot appreciate the true artificer, and admires Shakespeare for the wrong reasons. As he expatiates upon the weaknesses of the 'other' style of writing, Jonson fingers his own wounds.

(d) 'The Alchemist'

Having placed *De Shakespeare nostrati* in its immediate and in a larger context, we must return to *The Alchemist.* A recent editor compared 'To the Reader' with the allusion to Shakespeare in the Induction to *Bartholomew Fair (BF),* adding 'An attack on the taste of the period for 'romance' plays with scenes of spectacle in them is plain, but there is not the specific reference to Shakespeare seen in *BF*'[12]. I read the *Alchemist* epistle differently. The attack on 'romance' plays, I think, merely introduces Jonson's principal complaint, which is against ignorant, unskilful writers

who, 'to gain the opinion of copy' (copiousness, facility), utter all they
can; and this complaint inevitably implicates Shakespeare. Jonson distin-
guishes between fast writers, who presume 'on their own naturals', and
his own diligence, learning and polish – to achieve which he had to write
more slowly, and so was derided as 'barren, dull' or as 'a slow thing'[13].
An epistle printed with *The White Devil,* also in 1612, puts what appears
to have been a contemporary debate in its context.

> To those who report I was a long time in finishing this Tragedy, I
> confesse I do not write with a goose-quill, winged with two feathers
> . . . Detraction is the sworne friend to ignorance: For mine owne part I
> haue euer truly cherisht my good opinion of other mens worthy
> Labours, especially of that full and haightned stile of Maister *Chapman.*
> The labor'd and vnderstanding workes of Maister *Iohnson*: The no lesse
> worthy composures of the both worthily excellent Maister *Beamont,* &
> Maister *Fletcher*: And lastly (without wrong last to be named) the right
> happy and copious industry of M. *Shake-speare,* M. *Decker,* & M.
> *Heywood,* wishing what I write may be read by their light: Protesting,
> that, in the strength of mine owne iudgement, I know them so
> worthy, that though I rest silent in my owne worke, yet to most of
> theirs I dare (without flattery) fix that of *Martiall. – non norunt, Haec
> monumenta mori.*

Whether Webster's epistle preceded or followed Jonson's, it covers the
same ground. Webster, later to be ridiculed as 'crabbed Websterio'[14],
seems to have been a slow writer, like Jonson; nevertheless he insists that
the fast writers, Shakespeare, Dekker and Heywood, produced 'worthy
Labours' equal to Jonson's 'labor'd and vnderstanding workes'. This
looks like a peace-making exercise (Webster had formerly collaborated
with Dekker and Heywood, and knew what he was talking about). As
far as we are concerned, though, the epistle is chiefly interesting in
confirming that the 1612 debate about fast and laboured writers involved
Shakespeare. Webster named Shakespeare first of the fast writers; we may
take it that Jonson's principal target in 1612 was also Shakespeare – an
inference borne out by his repetition of the very same sentences in
Discoveries.

(e) 'Every Man Out Of His Humour'

Jonson's irritation, though not directed exclusively at one man,
repeatedly points at Shakespeare – even where he is not named. When

Jonson condemns fast writing or improbable plots, the immediate documentary context or the larger contemporary debate indicates a special sinner – the rival dramatist. If that is so, in the *Alchemist* epistle, in the essay on style that precedes and follows *De Shakespeare nostrati* in *Discoveries,* and in Jonson's agreed allusions to Shakespeare, we must take more seriously the possibility that the sneer in *Every Man Out Of His Humour* at improbable 'cross-wooing' comedies refers to *Twelfth Night.*

the argument of his *Comoedie* might haue beene of some other nature, as of a duke to be in loue with a countesse, and that countesse to bee in loue with the dukes sonne, and the sonne to loue the ladies waiting maid: some such crosse wooing, with a clowne to their seruingman . . .[15]

It is sometimes said that *Twelfth Night* was written just after *EMOH,* and could not be the target; the precise dates of both plays are uncertain, however, and at least one other passage in *EMOH* looks like a hit at *Twelfth Night.* '. . . of what yeeres is the knight, faire damsell? – GENT. Faith, much about your yeeres, sir. – PVNT. What complexion, or what stature beares he? – GENT. Of your stature, and very neere vpon your complexion. – PVNT. Mine is melancholy'[16]. Compare 'What kind of woman is't? *Viola.* Of your complexion. *Duke.* . . . What years, i'faith? *Viola.* About your years, my lord.' (*TN* ii. 4. 25ff.). Shakespeare, indeed, draws attention to the 'cross-wooing' in his play:

How will this fadge? My master loves her dearly,
And I, poor monster, fond as much on him;
And she, mistaken, seems to dote on me . . . (ii. 2. 31–33)

Before we decide about these possible allusions to *Twelfth Night* we should note that Jonson jeers at Shakespeare and his plays elsewhere in *EMOH.* '*Reason long since is fled to animals,* you know' (iii. 4. 33) (see p. 95, above) and probably '*Et tu Brute!*' (v. 6. 79) are hits at *Julius Caesar.* The first comes in the middle of a long satire against fools who purchase arms (iii. 2. 28), 'ramping to gentilitie' (iii. 4. 65); one, who has bought a 'ridiculous escutcheon', is told sarcastically 'Let the word bee, *Not without mustard*' (iii. 4. 86). (Shakespeare's newly acquired family 'word' was 'Non sanz droict'.) A choric commentator later says

let your imagination be swifter then a paire of oares: and by this, suppose *Puntaruolo, Briske, Fungoso,* and the dogge arriu'd at the court gate, and going vp to the great chamber. *Macilente,* and *Sogliardo,* wee'le leaue them on the water, till possibilitie and naturall meanes may land 'hem. Here come the gallants, now prepare your expectation. (IV. 8. 175ff.)

Here Jonson appears to ridicule Chorus in *Henry V,* with his repeated pleas to the audience (1) to take into account the 'due course of things' which cannot be properly presented, (2) to follow the king back and forth across the seas, (3) to use its imagination ('*Suppose* within the girdle of these walls ...', '*Suppose* that you have seen / The well-appointed King ...', '*Suppose* th' ambassador from the French comes back'). That Jonson was thinking of *Henry V* (a play dated 1599, like *Julius Caesar*) is confirmed by his later mockery of the chorus that 'wafts you ore the seas' (see p. 94, above).

Whether or not we believe that the 'cross-wooing' speech glances at *Twelfth Night,* EMOH bristles with allusions to Shakespeare (and, of course, to other writers) – right to the play's very last words, which are 'as fat, as Sir *Iohn Fal-Staffe*'. Most of these allusions are dismissive; and those that are not explicitly aimed at Jonson's rival are later repeated in more obviously 'Shakespearian' contexts. It is significant, I think, that Jonson's various critical charges were already formulated at this early date; and, equally, that Jonson said the same things so many times, almost as if he could not stop himself. The obsessive element in Jonson's criticism, which is most evident in *Discoveries* as he circles around Shakespeare while only naming him in one paragraph, also gives itself away, I feel, when Jonson, in a different context, employs arguments that might have been used against his own criticism of his rival. Writing EMOH, Jonson understood that a play might be 'strange, and of a particular kind by it selfe', not to be circumscribed by rules; classical authors enjoyed this freedom –

I see not then, but we should enioy the same licence, or free power, to illustrate and heighten our inuention as they did; and not to bee tyed to those strict and regular formes, which the nicenesse of a few ... would thrust vpon vs. (*Induction,* 231, 266ff.)

A quarter of a century later, he remained of the same opinion (*Discoveries,* 2555ff.), and yet he felt impelled to thrust upon Shakespeare 'strict and regular formes'. If Jonson could defend himself by claiming such licence, and by arguing that each play was unique, why not grant Shakespeare the same licence? Reluctantly we have to conclude that the sheer magnitude of Shakespeare's impact, or of his originality, clouded Jonson's judgment: only in the verses contributed to the first Folio could he rise above himself and discard his deeply-felt prejudice.

(f) The War of the Theatres

An account of the literary relations of Shakespeare and Jonson must not omit two other clashes that are less straightforward. First, the War of the Theatres, which I have already mentioned. That the two dramatists were on opposite sides is generally agreed; a speech by 'Kempe' to 'Burbage' in the third Cambridge *Parnassus* play (*c.* 1601) says so clearly enough.

> Why heres our fellow *Shakespeare* puts them all downe, I and *Ben Ionson* too. O that *Ben Ionson* is a pestilent fellow, he brought vp *Horace* giuing the Poets a pill, but our fellow *Shakespeare* hath giuen him a purge that made him beray his credit.

This refers to the emetic pill in *Poetaster* (1601); where, though, are we to locate Shakespeare's counter-purge? The most popular solution has been in *Troilus and Cressida*. *Poetaster* began, unusually, with a Prologue in armour; so did *Troilus* –

> ... and hither am I come
> A Prologue arm'd, but not in confidence
> Of author's pen or actor's voice ...

In addition Shakespeare remodelled Ajax, making him proud, covetous of praise, and childish – a more grotesque distortion of the Homeric original than the other Greeks and Trojans. Ajax promises to teach Achilles a lesson, 'I'll let his humours blood', and Agamemnon retorts, aside, 'He will be the physician that should be the patient' (II. 3. 208ff.), probably a side-swipe at Jonson's recent 'Humour' plays. Ulysses sarcastically flatters Ajax –

> Fam'd be thy tutor, and thy parts of nature
> Thrice-fam'd beyond, beyond all erudition (II. 3. 236–7)

– words that have little to do with Ajax's pretensions, but connect with Jonson's.

(g) Shakespeare's Sonnets

The *Sonnets* record a second, more fascinatingly elusive, clash about which there is far less agreement. A few nineteenth century critics thought that Jonson could have been the 'Rival Poet', without winning much support[17]. I believe that the case for Jonson is stronger than has been recognised, and, since no other obvious front-runner has emerged, should be looked at again. Thomas Fuller's note is the best starting point:

> Many were the *wit-combates* betwixt him and *Ben Iohnson,* which two I behold like a *Spanish great Gallion* and an *English man of War*; Master *Iohnson* (like the former) was built far higher in Learning; *Solid,* but *Slow* in his performances. *Shake-spear,* with the *English-man of War,* lesser in *bulk,* but lighter in *sailing,* could turn with all tides, tack about and take advantage of all winds, by the quickness of his Wit and Invention. (*Worthies,* 1662)[18]

Fuller, born in 1608, could just have witnessed a 'wit-combat' but, as Schoenbaum rightly says, 'the picture he had formed exists only in the mind's eye; this is a literary evocation, not a reminiscence derived from report'.[19] What, then, gave Fuller the idea? The answer seems to be Sonnet 80:

> O, how I faint when I of you do write,
> Knowing a better spirit doth use your name
> And in the praise thereof spends all his might
> To make me tongue-tied, speaking of your fame!
> But since your worth, wide as the ocean is,
> The humble as the proudest sail doth bear,
> My saucy bark, inferior far to his,
> On your broad main doth wilfully appear.
> Your shallowest help will hold me up afloat,
> Whilst he upon your soundless deep doth ride;
> Or, being wreck'd, I am a worthless boat,
> He of tall building and of goodly pride.
>   Then if he thrive, and I be cast away,
>   The worst was this: my love was my decay.

It has been said of Fuller that he described the wit-combats 'in terms reminiscent of the stock description of the Armada battle'[20]. This is true, yet the coincidence that Shakespeare and Fuller both resorted to Armada imagery cannot be explained as independent use of a common stock. How many other rivals in wit had been compared to war-ships? Of how many others would it have been true that one was learned, the other 'unlettered'? –

> My tongue-tied Muse in manners holds her still,
> While comments of your praise, richly compil'd,
> Reserve their character with golden quill
> And precious phrase by all the Muses fil'd.
> I think good thoughts, whilst other write good words,
> And, like unlettered clerk, still cry 'Amen'
> To every hymn that able spirit affords
> In polish'd form of well-refined pen. (Sonnet 85)

The idea that Shakespeare was 'unlettered' lurks beneath several of Jonson's sarcasms about the plays, and came into the open in the Folio verses ('And though thou hadst small *Latine,* and lesse *Greeke*'); and several seventeenth century anecdotes suggest Shakespeare's awareness of Jonson's attitude – for example, his offer to give his god-son, Jonson's son, a generous christening present: 'I faith *Ben:* I'le e'en giue him a douzen good Lattin Spoones, and thou shalt translate them'[21] (*latten:* a mixed metal, brass, i.e not the more customary silver spoons; *translate:* punning on the sense 'transform' (*OED* 4), i.e. translate them into silver). Again we have to ask – who else, apart from Jonson, could be so overbearing as to make Shakespeare feel 'worthless' and 'unlettered' in comparison[22]? The *pride* of the rival poet, like Ajax's pride in *Troilus and Cressida,* mentioned in Sonnet 80, reappears in Sonnet 86:

> Was it the proud full sail of his great verse,
> Bound for the prize of all-too-precious you,
> That did my ripe thoughts in my brain inhearse,
> Making their tomb the womb wherein they grew?
> Was it his spirit, by spirits taught to write
> Above a mortal pitch, that struck me dead?
> No, neither he, nor his compeers by night
> Giving him aid, my verse astonished.

Jonson fits the allusions in the sonnets quite remarkably. The alert reader, however, has noticed a difficulty: Fuller spoke of Jonson as slow and ponderous in the wit-combats, implying that quick-witted Shakespeare made rings round him – whereas the poet of the sonnets more than once describes himself as 'tongue-tied', 'struck dead' by his rival. The explanation, I think, lies in the special circumstance that Shakespeare had imagined himself the Young Man's favourite poet; when a determined rival appears on the scene and 'spends all his might / To make me tongue-tied' (80. 3–4), i.e. tries to crush Shakespeare, the Young Man feels free to encourage the newcomer, who is also a good poet – and Shakespeare, hurt, decides not to compete. Not the rival's quickwittedness but the Young Man's insensitivity silenced Shakespeare, as he spelt out in the conclusion of Sonnet 86.

> He nor that affable familiar ghost
> Which nightly gulls him with intelligence,
> As victors, of my silence cannot boast:
> I was not sick of any fear from thence.
>> But when your countenance fill'd up his line,
>> Then lack'd I matter; that enfeebled mine.

If Jonson is the rival poet the sonnets do not really contradict Fuller, since Shakespeare implies (i) that he is not usually tongue-tied, (ii) that he had much to say, but chose not to say it. The tradition of 'wit-combats', confirmed by others apart from Fuller[23], fits in with the rivalry described in the sonnets, even though a special 'triangle' situation for once produced an unexpected outcome.

Jonson's claim to be the rival poet may help us to identify the Young Man. Contemporary records associate Shakespeare with only three noble patrons – the earls of Southampton, Pembroke, and Montgomery. Jonson courted the last two, particularly Pembroke, to whom he dedicated *Catiline* and his *Epigrams;* Pembroke, for his part, recommended Jonson for the honorary degree of Master of Arts at Oxford, and sent him £20 every New Year's Day. Is it a mere coincidence that William Herbert, Earl of Pembroke, the patron of Jonson, Shakespeare's only important literary 'rival', had the initials 'W. H.' – or is it a priceless clue? It depends on what we make of the dedication of the Sonnets. I believe that this dedication, signed 'T. T.' (i.e. Thomas Thorpe, the publisher), adapts one found in the manuscript and written by the poet. Here are (a) the printed version, and (b) a reconstruction of the MS. original.

(a) TO. THE. ONLIE. BEGETTER. OF.
THESE. INSUING. SONNETS.
MR. W. H. ALL. HAPPINESSE.
AND. THAT. ETERNITIE.
PROMISED.

BY.
OUR. EVER-LIVING. POET.
WISHETH.
THE. WELL-WISHING.
ADVENTURER. IN.
SETTING.
FORTH.

T. T.

(b) TO. THE. ONLIE. BEGETTER. OF.
THESE. INSUING. SONNETS.
W. H.
ALL. HAPPINESSE.
AND. THAT. ETERNITIE.
PROMISED.
BY.
THE. POET.

W. S.

A bold assertion? Yes, but supported by an interesting verbal echo. The phrase 'all happiness', not at all common in dedications, also occurs in the dedication of *Lucrece* (1594): '. . . Were my worth greater my duety would shew greater, meane time, as it is, it is bound to your Lordship; To whom I wish long life still lengthned with all happinesse.' While the second half of (b) is little more than a possibility, the first four lines, incorporating as they do a Shakespearian phrase, seem to me to have a good claim to represent the original. And if the dedicatee[24] figured simply as 'W. H.', what would be more natural than that the printer should attach the obvious title to an unknown dignitary who is not identified by the poet as either a lord or a knight? Shakespeare had his reasons for not giving away the Young Man's identity; printed dedications, on the other hand, traditionally so fulsome in describing the dedicatee, could not do without titles.

(h) The Shakespeare mythos

Finally, the Shakespeare 'mythos' deserves a moment's attention. Though we must not make too much of it, it confirms that the two dramatists were connected in the popular mind and that their rivalry was taken for granted. Stories of wit-combats, of Jonson's epitaph completed by Shakespeare, of the latten spoons for Jonson's child, all too often turn on Jonson's competitiveness and Shakespeare's easy superiority. When

Rowe first told (in 1709) how Shakespeare 'luckily cast his eye' upon a Jonson play that the actors were about to refuse, and recommended it, the same note is heard. 'After this they were profess'd Friends; tho' I don't know whether the other ever made him an equal return of Gentleness, and Sincerity'. By now Jonson's malice was part of the 'mythos', as can be seen from Dryden's description – unfair, I think – of Jonson's verses for the first Folio as 'An Insolent, Sparing, and invidious Panegyrick'[25]. Whether myth or fact, this view dates from Jonson's life-time: in his verses for the Folio and in 'De Shakespeare nostrati', his two most important comments, he found it necessary to deny his supposed malice[26]. All the more likely, therefore, that Jonson was the rival poet of the *Sonnets,* the one important rival complained of by Shakespeare himself.

*   *   *

In the adverse criticism of Shakespeare the writer published by his contemporaries there are two surprises. First, that – with one exception – so few of them went in for fault-finding, in an age when so many plays (including Shakespeare's) contained unkind reflections on the work of other dramatists. Second, that the exception, Ben Jonson, had so much more to say than was previously known. Even if we discount the suggestion that Jonson was the rival poet of the *Sonnets,* which has lain dormant for too long and needs further scrutiny, Jonson's opposition to his great rival was sustained and irrepressible. I have concentrated on the comments that still require annotation – those in *Discoveries,* in the *Alchemist* epistle, in *EMOH* – and have said little about others. Whether we explain them as malice, obsession, friendly rivalry, or as a neo-classical hangover – or as a combination of some or all of these – they add up to a body of criticism that could not be ignored[27].

6
Shakespeare's Reply to Criticism

Jonson's criticisms, I repeat, could not be ignored. How did Shakespeare deal with the situation? Looking at the dates of the various comments one might be tempted to argue that the situation remained bottled up in Jonson's brooding mind until Shakespeare retired to Stratford in 1611, and created no problems. Although Jonson's attitude appears to be fully defined in *Every Man Out Of His Humour* (1599), the tone here is mostly good-natured: *Poetaster* (1601), if it refers to Shakespeare at all, does so only glancingly; and the Prologue to *Every Man In His Humour*, where Jonson presses his case more sharply, while usually dated 1605, may be as late as 1612. The first criticism that shows resentment is the epistle 'To the Reader' printed with *The Alchemist* (1612); perhaps, then, Jonson courteously – or diplomatically – refrained from speaking out until his rival had departed from London.

Such an explanation would totally disregard Jonson's temperament. We know from the War of the Theatres, and from other sources, that Drummond's summing-up hit the mark: 'He [Jonson] is a great lover and praiser of himself, a contemner and Scorner of others, given rather to losse a friend, than a Jest, jealous of every word and action of those about him . . .'[1]. Is it likely that a man so aggressive and outspoken would remain silent about the 'ridiculous' lines in *Julius Caesar* and the other 'ill customes' of its author? When Inigo Jones accused Jonson 'for naming him behind his back a foole he denied it but sayes he. I said he was ane arrant knave & I avouch it'[2]. The London taverns must have heard Jonson express his views, in his forthright way – drink, said Drummond, 'is one of the Elements jn which he liveth' – and Shakespeare could scarcely have failed to be aware of them. If there were merry meetings and wit-combats, what more probable than that Jonson would air his grievances? He 'would not flatter though he saw Death,' said Drummond; 'he is passionately kynde and angry, carelesse either to gaine or keep'[3].

Let us assume that Jonson knew before Shakespeare retired what displeased him in the plays, and spoke out. Since he repeated himself so much later, it is not difficult to guess what he would have said. He disliked romantic, improbable plots that stray too far from 'deedes, and language, such as men doe vse'; he saw himself as the champion of 'nature', chiding those who 'runne away from Nature' (*Alchemist*, epistle), being himself 'loth to make Nature afraid in his *Playes*, like those that beget *Tales, Tempests*, and such like *Drolleries*' (*Bartholomew Fair*), and unwilling to 'run away from nature, as [if] hee were afraid of her; or depart from life, and the likenesse of Truth' (*Discoveries*, iv (d))[4]. As the last quotation shows, 'nature' also meant 'life' and 'truth'; Jonson, in short, here still advocates the principles long ago enunciated in *EMOH*, where, after ridiculing 'cross-wooing' comedies, he had proposed as the alternative Cicero's definition − 'who would haue a *Comoedie*, to be *Imitatio vitae, Speculum consuetudinis, Imago veritatis*' (III. 6. 204−7). The watchwords were Nature, Life and Truth.

Back, then, to our original question. Assuming that Jonson spoke out − and it would be uncharacteristic of him not to − how would Shakespeare deal with the situation? As I have suggested elsewhere, he did not ignore the other principal charge against him, that he wrote too much 'bombast'; instead, he resorted to a very simple expedient − he got in with it first.

> In *Hamlet* Shakespeare does not defend heightened speech and improbable action; he merely intimates, again and again, that he *knows* that what he writes sounds like wild and whirling words, or croaking, prating, mouthing, ranting, roaring, thunder, passionate speech, horrid speech, antic or distempered language, tearing a passion to tatters. Doing this he partly disarms criticism; he takes the 'bombast' out of its sails.[5]

So, too, when he was accused of violating Nature, Life and Truth. Unless the evidence has disappeared, he composed no inductions, prologues or epilogues, or epistles to the reader, to defend himself. But in one of his late plays he intimates, again and again, that he knows that what he writes appears to flout Nature, Life and Truth; he counter-attacks by laughing at the simple-minded who think they can grasp such slippery concepts, and, more surprisingly, twice more or less halts the play to offer a reasoned reply to his critics.

Unlike Jonson, Shakespeare seems not to have felt drawn to literary theory. We learn from *A Midsummer Night's Dream*, however, that he knew how to deal with hard-headed theorists who believed in Nature, Life and Truth − for, as I have mentioned, Jonson's criticisms of

Shakespeare continued an earlier debate[6]. Theseus represents the Jonsonian view; he refuses to believe 'fables' and 'fairy toys', the fantasies of seething brains that create 'More than cool reason ever comprehends.'

> The lunatic, the lover, and the poet,
> Are of imagination all compact.
> One sees more devils than vast hell can hold;
> That is the madman. The lover, all as frantic,
> Sees Helen's beauty in a brow of Egypt.
> The poet's eye, in a fine frenzy rolling,
> Doth glance from heaven to earth, from earth to heaven;
> And as imagination bodies forth
> The forms of things unknown, the poet's pen
> Turns them to shapes, and gives to airy nothing
> A local habitation and a name. (v. 1. 7.ff.)

The joke is, of course, that the audience has actually witnessed the 'fairy toys' so solemnly denied by Theseus: he thinks them 'airy nothing', the fantasies of the poet's frenzy, 'more strange than true', whereas the audience knows them to be 'true' within the framework of the play.

Rather than justify himself by addressing the audience, Shakespeare adopted a less ham-fisted strategy. He merely hinted that the 'bombast' in *Hamlet* serves a purpose; he slyly let Theseus condemn himself out of his own mouth. In short, he trusted the audience to see his point of view. Towards the end of his career, however, he decided on a different course – perhaps because his only persistent critic, Ben Jonson, had gained in confidence and was persuading supporters that Shakespeare's plays (running away from Nature, Life and Truth) need not be taken too seriously.

The play in which Shakespeare replies to Jonson is *The Winter's Tale* (1611). Polixenes, in the sheep-shearing scene, returns to the underlying theme of Theseus' speech – the 'truth' of art. Perdita had explained that she prefers not to grow slips (cuttings) of 'carnations and streak'd gillyvors'.

> *Polixenes*   Wherefore, gentle maiden,
> Do you neglect them?
> *Perdita*   For I have heard it said
> There is an art which in their piedness shares
> With great creating nature.
> *Polixenes*   Say there be;

> Yet nature is made better by no mean
> But nature makes that mean; so over that art,
> Which you say adds to nature, is an art,
> That nature makes. You see, sweet maid, we marry
> A gentler scion to the wildest stock,
> And make conceive a bark of baser kind
> By bud of nobler race. This is an art
> Which does mend nature – change it rather: but
> The art itself is nature. (IV. 4. 85ff.)

Where Jonson invoked Cicero's definition to condemn art that runs away from nature and truth, Shakespeare falls back on the customary Renaissance defence, that art is the agent of nature and operates within nature's domain. 'Tha art itself is nature.'

How can we be so certain, though, that Polixenes' speech, ostensibly about gardening, should be understood as a reply to Jonson? It follows shortly after a formal defence of the play's departure from 'truth' and 'nature' – its leap across sixteen years – and picks up the same argument.

ENTER TIME, THE CHORUS.

> *Time* I, that please some, try all, both joy and terror
> Of good and bad, that makes and unfolds error,
> Now take upon me, in the name of Time,
> To use my wings. Impute it not a crime
> To me or my swift passage that I slide
> O'er sixteen years, and leave the growth untried
> Of that wide gap, since it is in my power
> To o'erthrow law, and in one self-born hour
> To plant and o'erwhelm custom ... (IV. 1. 1ff.)

According to 'Cicero's definition' comedy should be an imitation of life, a mirror of *custom,* an image of truth. Time informs us that 'custom' is not fixed and unchangeable, as Polixenes later argues that nature must not be seen as unchangeable, – so why call it a crime when the dramatist adjusts custom and nature to suit his purposes? Although Shakespeare stops short of saying so, he is on the brink of arguing that all drama, and not just his own, must 'overthrow law' and run away from nature, if one accepts Jonson's definitions; Jonson's plays are as guilty as his own, except that they observe their own laws (of language, construction, 'humours' etc.). Coming so soon after Time's authorial self-justification

– which may, indeed, have been spoken by Shakespeare himself –
Polixenes' speech, developing the same ideas, is something more than an
innocent digression on the art of gardening.

Time and Polixenes speak for Shakespeare, and do so with an
unaccustomed seriousness. But Shakespeare's 'reply' also slips into
playfulness, the sly mockery that we noticed in *A Midsummer Night's
Dream*, the characteristic of his 'wit-combats' as described by Fuller: he
'could turn with all tides, tack about and take advantage of all winds, by
the quickness of his Wit and Invention.' A hundred and fifty lines after
Polixenes' speech Shakespeare saw an opening, and mercilessly derided
those who insist on truth in literature.

> *Mopsa* Pray now, buy some. I love a ballad in print a-life, for then we
> are sure they are true.
> *Autolycus* Here's one to a very doleful tune: how a usurer's wife was
> brought to bed of twenty money-bags at a burden, and how she long'd
> to eat adders' heads and toads carbonado'd.
> *Mopsa* Is it true, think you?
> *Autolycus* Very true, and but a month old.
> *Dorcas* Bless me from marrying a usurer!
> *Autolycus* Here's the midwife's name to't, one Mistress Taleporter, and
> five or six honest wives that were present. Why should I carry lies
> abroad? ... Here's another ballad, of a fish that appeared upon the
> coast on Wednesday the fourscore of April, forty thousand fathom
> above water, and sung this ballad against the hard hearts of maids. It
> was thought she was a woman, and was turned into a cold fish for she
> would not exchange flesh with one that lov'd her. The ballad is very
> pitiful, and as true.
> *Dorcas* Is it true too, think you?
> *Autolycus* Five justices' hands at it; and witnesses more than my pack
> will hold. (IV. 4. 256ff.)

So much for *imago veritatis*! Is an improbable tale more likely to be true
because a midwife and six honest wives, or five justices, are said to vouch
for it? Is that Jonson's 'truth'? 'What *is* truth?' asks jesting Shakespeare
– and, if we have ears to hear, provides an answer that differs profoundly
from Jonson's.

It is characteristic of Shakespeare's teasing indirectness that he invites
us, if we are so inclined, to think of him, the author of *The Winter's Tale*,
as 'Mistress Taleporter.' He had teased the audience before, in a similar
way, when Hermione asked her young son, Mamillius, to 'tell us a tale.'

> *Mamillius* Merry or sad shall't be?
> *Hermione* As merry as you will.
> *Mamillius* A sad tale's best for winter. I have one
> Of sprites and goblins. (ɪɪ. 1. 23ff.)

Alluding thus to the play's title, Shakespeare encourages us to believe that 'the winter's tale' will be nothing more than a 'winter-tale' (i.e. an old wives' tale). Mistress Taleporter sets the same booby-trap for us towards the end, when we look back at the play's events with the principals of the story. 'This news, which is called true, is so like an old tale that the verity of it is in strong suspicion. Has the King found his heir? — Most true, if ever truth were pregnant by circumstance' (v. 2. 27ff.). Twice more Shakespeare rubs in the point that his story resembles an 'old tale', each time drawing attention to its improbability. 'What, pray you, became of Antigonus? ... Like an old tale still ... he was torn to pieces with a bear.' And —

> That she is living,
> Were it but told you, should be hooted at
> Like an old tale; but it appears she lives.

In these passages Shakespeare throws a challenge to the audience, suggesting that what appears to be no more than an 'old tale' may nevertheless be in some sense 'true'. Inside the play the 'old tale' events are certainly as true as the characters who feel that 'the verity of it is in strong suspicion' (this is the strategy of *A Midsummer Night's Dream*), yet when we look at the same events from outside the play, as theatre-goers, can we still defend them as 'true'?

The play's questioning of Nature, Life and Truth climaxes in the statue-scene. It has been said that this is the one and only instance where Shakespeare cheats his audience: Paulina and Antigonus had spoken of Hermione as dead, the audience believes her dead, and suddenly she stands there, she stirs, she lives! In a play in which Shakespeare defends the dramatist's right to disregard law and custom, it is surely no accident that everything converges upon a 'marvel' that defies all rational explanation. Critics have solemnly disputed whether we are to suppose that a statue is magically brought to life, or that a middle-aged queen pretends to be a statue — missing the point that Shakespeare has quite deliberately arranged things so that we cannot tell. While Hermione stands still and silent, the two explanations are equally plausible and implausible; because we cannot decide between them the woman-statue or statue-woman is, as far as we are concerned, outside Life as we know it. In these moments of suspense it is *sui generis,* unique, a 'marvel'. Strangely, though, we do not repudiate it as a gross imposture, an impossibility to be hooted at. On the contrary, the emotion generated by Leontes and Perdita normally grips the theatre-audience as well, an intoxicating conviction that the impossible can and must happen: and as we surrender to this feeling we give our assent to the story, we believe in it on its own terms, discarding all preconceptions about Nature, Life and Truth.

Shakespeare added the statue-scene to the story (adapted from Greene's *Pandosto*) for several good reasons. One was, I think, that the statue, when no one knows what to make of it, perfectly represents the challenge of a new work of art – an experience that is always *sui generis,* a mystery. The statue that becomes Hermione is the quintessential art-work, involving sculpture, painting, music, drama – and as we participate in Leontes' wonder, and in the 'magic' of the experience, our response to the statue channels our response to the play, the one melting into the other. Not only the statue but the art-experience that now draws to an end defies rational explanation and affects us, to echo the words of those caught up in it, as a thing of wonder and amazement.

It is required, says Paulina to her audience, that 'you do awake your faith'; the art-work will 'Strike all that look upon with marvel.' Shakespeare speaks through her to the theatre-audience, asking it to accept what he offers as a kind of magic, to be tested not by cool reason but by an act of faith. Here, then, we have his reply to Nature, Life and Truth – an alternative critical theory that may be summarised as Wonder, Magic and Faith. Having laughed at Jonson's 'truth' in the Autolycus-ballads episode, having hinted several times that his own 'old tale' is in a sense true ('Why should I carry lies abroad?') Shakespeare finally abandons any claim to truth, and steers to a conclusion more complicated than Keats' famous compromise that Beauty is Truth ('I am certain of nothing but of the holiness of the heart's affections, and the truth of Imagination. What the Imagination seizes as Beauty must be Truth'); in effect he appears to anticipate more modern thinking about the autonomy of the work of art, and to imply that the work of art cannot be certified 'true' from outside but must validate itself from within.

If Shakespeare drops the claim to truth so completely, it may be said, why does he take the trouble to explain the statue retrospectively? Is this not a relapse, an unnecessary clutching at the criteria of Life and Truth? Hermione tells Perdita that

> thou shalt hear that I,
> Knowing by Paulina that the oracle
> Gave hope thou wast in being, have preserv'd
> Myself to see the issue.

So the statue was after all a woman pretending to be a statue! The explanation, however, achieves very little if its purpose is to bring the story within the boundaries of Life and Truth; quite the contrary, for women do not normally pretend to be statues, nor can we believe that loving wives in our bread-and-butter world would live for sixteen years so near to a heart-broken husband without lifting the telephone (or the Jacobean equivalent). The explanation that Hermione preserved herself, etc., is in line with other seemingly life-like features of the play – a jealous husband, a man-eating bear – not one of which affects us as 'the real thing'; they may be life-like but are not Life, since the dramatist so shapes each episode, and the whole, that we never lose sight of the fact that we are watching Art, not Life. The play's many life-like moments, that is to say, keep it in touch with Life without actually being an appeal to Life to validate what it presents; like an aeroplane flying through cloud, the play allows us to glimpse Land now and then, we have the reassuring sense that we are still in contact with Life, and all the while we are up in the clouds, in a self-contained world.

Hermione's explanation fleetingly gives us our bearings; she is not to be seen as a dummy, pushed aside and then set up again by totally arbitrary artists (Paulina; Shakespeare), but as a human being with her own reasons, her own continuity. Shakespeare evidently felt that a glimpse of 'Life' at this point was indispensable and that a mere glimpse was enough. Romance, not Life, exerts the strongest pull at the end; the patient wife who waits for years before she returns to her penitent husband is borrowed, like the statue, from Romance – and, as if to put it beyond all doubt that he repudiates Nature, Life and Truth, Shakespeare magically pulls out of his sleeve a pair of old turtles, Paulina and Camillo, a love-match entirely unprepared for and as improbable as the statue itself.

Although romance is in the ascendant at the end, it would be wrong to suggest that romance pure and simple is the Shakespearian package offered as an alternative to Jonson's 'deedes, and language, such as men doe vse'. Let us go back once more to the statue. There are many signs that Shakespeare prepared for this master-stroke by bringing the story into contact with the Proserpina-myth; Perdita wants to dispense flowers to all, like a spring-goddess, like Proserpina –

O Proserpina,
For the flowers now that, frighted, thou let'st fall
From Dis's waggon! – daffodils,
That come before the swallow dares, and take
The winds of March with beauty; violets, dim
But sweeter than the lids of Juno's eyes . . . (IV. 4. 116ff.)

When Antigonus abandons Perdita as an infant, he says '*Blossom,* speed thee well!' (III. 3. 46), an unusual word for a child; when Perdita and Florizel (her flower prince) meet Leontes in Act V he welcomes them as if they are the spring – 'Welcome hither / As is *the spring* to th'earth' (V. 1. 151). In these and other passages Shakespeare presents Perdita as a Proserpina-figure; and Proserpina's mother, of course, was Ceres, the goddess of fertility, who, when Dis (Pluto, the god of the underworld) snatched away her daughter, 'went ranging vp and downe the world to finde her.' According to the myth, all growth stopped in Ceres' absence; Jupiter then decreed that Dis must restore Proserpina to Ceres for so many months every year, and, when this happens, Ceres ceases to mourn for her, exerts her benign influence again, and spring returns to the world. 'By the person of *Ceres,*' explained Leonard Digges (for whom see p. 38), 'is signified *Tillage.* By *Proserpine,* the seedes which are sowed, by *Pluto,* the earth that receiues them'[8]. The myth, expounded in editions of Ovid that Shakespeare must have used at school, and in *The Tempest* (IV. 1. 76ff.), suggested 'the *winter's* tale' (winter being the life-denying passion of Leontes), and, if we have been properly attentive, also introduced its resonances in the concluding scene, when a daughter is restored to her mother and the mother returns to the world, the statue stirs – bringing a spring-like joy to all.

While I do not wish to propose that 'Hermione is Ceres', we may say that the Proserpina myth, another view from the aeroplane, also helps to give us our bearings. Myth, at certain points, knits with romance, breathes new significances into it; 'we marry', to quote Shakespeare's own words, 'A gentler scion to the wildest stock.' Grafting-imagery, however, fails to suggest the multiple hybridisation that occurs in the plays. Paulina's unexpected betrothal to Camillo cannot be called romance pure and simple, because romance looked down its nose at the love-longings of the elderly (such as Basileus and Gynecia in the *Arcadia*), and old turtles introduce an element of comedy. *The Winter's Tale,* of course, concludes with *two* pairs of elderly lovers, and Shakespeare, it seems, so far from wishing to exclude comedy, as lesser artists might have done, quite deliberately made room for anti-romantic touches of comic realism.

> Hermione was not so much wrinkled . . .
> The ruddiness upon her lip is wet . . .
> When she was young you woo'd her; now in age
> Is she become the suitor?

The Shakespearian package, in short, brings together life, romance, myth, comedy, and much else besides — a different mixture in every play, so that every play presents its own unique challenge, its own magic, like the mysterious statue.

The Winter's Tale, I believe, contains a comprehensive reply to Jonson's charge that Shakespeare's plays run away from Nature, Life and Truth. Shakespeare's next two plays appear to refer back to the same debate: *The Tempest* ostentatiously observed the neo-classical unities, his first to do so since *The Comedy of Errors* — almost as if to say 'I can play the game according to *your* rules, but it's still *my* kind of art'; and *Henry VIII*, again, obliquely mocked the opposition by claiming truth, Jonson's truth, in its original title. 'The King's players,' wrote Wotton, 'had a new play, called *All is True,* representing some principal pieces of the reign of Henry VIII . . .' As far as Jonson was concerned, though, *The Winter's Tale* must have had the greatest impact as a reply; and I suspect that he was thinking specifically of this play in the querulous epistle added to *The Alchemist* in 1612 (for which see p. 98). Jonson disliked 'Daunces and Antickes', and the antic *'Dance of twelve Satyrs'*, that 'gallimaufry of gambols' (*WT* IV. 4. 318ff.) was an obvious offender; after mentioning dramatists that 'runne away from Nature' he rebuked professors of art who 'are growne so obstinate contemners of it' that they, 'by simple mocking at the termes, when they vnderstand not the things, thinke to get of wittily with their Ignorance.' That could be Jonson's countercuff to Polixenes' speech ('The art itself is nature'), and to Mrs Taleporter's 'true' ballads. 'I deny not,' Jonson conceded, 'but that these men . . . may some time happen on some thing that is good, and great.' What other dramatist of the opposing camp could wring out of Jonson an acknowledgement that his writing might be 'good, and great', apart from Shakespeare? 'I know,' Jonson continued, 'if it were put to the question of theirs, and mine, the worse would finde more suffrages.' Who else could be described as more popular than Jonson in 1612, not long after the success of *The Alchemist,* apart from Shakespeare? The language of the epistle is veiled, either because Shakespeare still visited London in 1612 or because Jonson knew that he might be accused of malice, but there can be little doubt that, once again, it was Jonson's chief professional rival who had provoked him. While some of the charges in the epistle may point at other men as well, several point first and foremost at Shakespeare, taken on their own; it is equally significant, though, that no other single dramatist can be Jonson's target, if the charges are taken together. No other dramatist had (i) publicly mocked Jonson's 'termes', *and* (ii) earned his admiration as sometimes 'good, and great', *and* (iii) attracted a popular following that roused his envy, *and* (iv) included 'Daunces and Antickes' in a recent play.

Several chapters in this book have been concerned with Jonson's comments on Shakespeare. Jonson is, without question, our most valuable single source of information for the study of Shakespeare's contemporary impact; and of all Jonson's comments I find the *Alchemist* epistle the most fascinating. The poem written for the first Folio is a magnificent tribute but, like the note 'De Shakespeare nostrati', it looks back at a great man from a fixed point of view – that of a friend and rival who now admits that 'the wonder of our Stage' outshone all competitors. In the *Alchemist* epistle, on the other hand, we can observe the dramatists locked in argument, a 'wit-combat' such as Fuller described, before Jonson accepted that he could not match the other's achievement. Only forty years old, Jonson could not know that just one more great play would come from his pen. He had staked his claims with brilliant early comedies, followed by *Volpone, Epicoene, The Alchemist*; he fervently believed in his tragedies, even though the 'ignorant' had not understood them; he had composed a much more varied collection of occasional verse than Shakespeare, had dazzled with his court masques, a *genre* not attempted by his rival, he was befriended by the aristocracy. At this stage in his career, when some of Shakespeare's best plays could not be studied in printed texts, Jonson might not unreasonably think of himself as Shakespeare's equal as a writer, and as superior in learning. Yet, though elsewhere brimful of self-confidence, he adopted a very different tone in the *Alchemist* epistle – and it is this tone that I find fascinating. Querulous, even angry, it has the smell of defeat about it. Jonson expresses scorn for the adversary's inferior wares, yet cannot disguise the fact that he struggles against formidable opposition: 'presumers on their owne Naturalls ... deriders of all diligence ... [they] thinke to get of wittily with their Ignorance.' Is this not the very picture suggested by Fuller?

Master *Iohnson* ... built far higher in Learning; *Solid,* but *Slow* in his performances. *Shake-spear,* with the *English-man of War,* lesser in *bulk,* but lighter in *sailing,* could turn with all tides, tack about and take advantage of all winds, by the quickness of his Wit and Invention.

We see from *The Winter's Tale* how teasingly elusive and quick and sharp the older man could be; and the *Alchemist* epistle, I believe, reveals how the '*Spanish great Gallion*' reacted under fire. All the more credit to Jonson that, after Shakespeare's death, he wrote so movingly of 'my beloved'! And who but Shakespeare could have handled so difficult a rival so expertly, firmly putting him in his place without making an enemy of him?

Although we hear so much from Jonson about Shakespeare, a mystery remains. What was Shakespeare's private opinion of Jonson? If Jonson could later say 'I loved the man', it is natural to assume that, wit-combats notwithstanding, the two dramatists sometimes enjoyed each other's company. Yet, though Shakespeare remembered many friends in his will, including his London colleagues Burbage, Heminge and Condell, he left nothing to Jonson. I deduce that in 1616 Shakespeare did not greatly 'love the man'; perhaps (who could blame him?) he now agreed with the words put in the mouth of Will Kempe in the third *Parnassus* play of 1601—

O that *Ben Ionson* is a pestilent fellow!

Appendix A

Selected Contemporary Allusions

1. Robert Greene, *Groats-Worth of Witte* (1592). Quoted and discussed above, pp. 1–6, 53–4. See also Appendix B.
2. Henry Chettle, *Kind-Harts Dreame* (1592; SR 8 Dec. 1592), from the Epistle, 'To the Gentlemen Readers'. Discussed pp. 7, 21.

> he that offendes being forst, is more excusable than the wilfull faultie
> . . . Ile shew reason for my present writing, and after proceed to sue for
> pardon. About three moneths since died *M. Robert Greene*, leauing
> many papers in sundry Booke sellers hands, among other his Groats-
> worth of wit, in which a letter written to diuers play-makers, is
> offensiuely by one or two of them taken, and because on the dead they
> cannot be auenged, they wilfully forge in their conceites a liuing
> Author: and after tossing it two and fro, no remedy, but it must light
> on me. How I haue all the time of my conuersing in printing hindred
> the bitter inueying against schollers, it hath been very well knowne,
> and how in that I dealt I can sufficiently prooue. With neither of them
> that take offence was I acquainted, and with one of them I care not if I
> neuer be: The other [i.e. Shakespeare], whome at that time I did not so
> much spare, as since I wish I had, for that as I haue moderated the
> heate of liuing writers, and might haue vsde my owne discretion
> (especially in such a case) the Author beeing dead, that I did not, I am
> as sory, as if the originall fault had beene my fault, because my selfe
> haue seene his demeanor no lesse ciuill than he exelent in the qualitie he
> professes: Besides, diuers of worship haue reported, his vprightnes of
> dealing, which argues his honesty, and his facetious grace in writting,
> that aprooues his Art.[1]

3. Francis Meres, *Palladis Tamia: Wits Treasury* (1598). Discussed pp. 43, 75–6.

As the soule of *Euphorbus* was thought to liue in *Pythagoras*: so the sweete wittie soule of *Ouid* liues in mellifluous & hony-tongued *Shakespeare*, witnes his *Venus* and *Adonis*, his *Lucrece*, his sugred Sonnets among his priuate friends, &c.

As *Plautus* and *Seneca* are accounted the best for Comedy and Tragedy among the Latines: so *Shakespeare* among the English is the most excellent in both kinds for the stage; for Comedy, witnes his *Gentlemen of Verona*, his *Errors*, his *Loue labors lost*, his *Loue labours wonne*, his *Midsummers night dreame*, & his *Merchant of Venice*: for Tragedy his *Richard the 2. Richard the 3. Henry the 4. King Iohn, Titus Andronicus* and his *Romeo* and *Iuliet*.

As *Epius Stolo* said, that the Muses would speake with *Plautus* tongue, if they would speak Latin: so I say that the Muses would speak with *Shakespeares* fine filed phrase, if they would speake English ...

These are our best for Tragedie, the Lorde *Buckhurst*, Doctor *Leg* of Cambridge, Doctor *Edes* of Oxforde, maister *Edward Ferris*, the Authour of the *Mirrour for Magistrates, Marlow, Peele, Watson, Kid, Shakespeare, Drayton, Chapman, Decker*, and *Beniamin Iohnson* ...

The best for Comedy amongst vs bee, *Edward* Earle of Oxforde, Doctor *Gager* of Oxforde, Maister *Rowley* once a rare Scholler of learned Pembrooke Hall in Cambridge, Maister *Edwardes* one of her Maiesties Chappell, eloquent and wittie *Iohn Lilly, Lodge, Gascoyne, Greene, Shakespeare, Thomas Nash, Thomas Heywood, Anthony Mundye* our best plotter, *Chapman, Porter, Wilson, Hathway*, and *Henry Chettle* ...

4. Anonymous, Epistle to the reader, in *Troilus and Cressida* (1609, second issue). Discussed p. 43.

A neuer writer, to an euer
reader. Newes.

Eternall reader, you haue heere a new play, neuer stal'd with the Stage, neuer clapper-clawd with the palmes of the vulger, and yet passing full of the palme comicall; for it is a birth of your braine, that neuer vndertooke any thing commicall, vainely: And were but the vaine names of commedies changde for the titles of Commodities, or of Playes for Pleas; you should see all those grand censors, that now stile them such vanities, flock to them for the maine grace of their grauities: especially this authors Commedies, that are so fram'd to the life, that they serue for the most common Commentaries, of all the actions of our liues shewing such a dexteritie, and power of witte, that the most displeased with Playes, are pleasd with his Commedies. And all such dull and heauy-witted worldlings, as were neuer capable of the witte of a Commedie, comming by report of them to his representations, haue found that witte there, that they neuer found in them-selues, and haue parted better wittied then they came: feeling an edge of witte set vpon them, more than euer they dreamd they had braine to grinde it on. So much and such sauored salt of witte is in his Commedies that they seeme (for their height of pleasure) to be borne in that sea that brought forth *Venus*. Amongst all there is none more witty then this: And had I time I would comment vpon it, though I know it needs not, (for so much as will make you thinke your testerne well bestowd) but for so much worth, as euen poore I know to be stuft in it. It deserues such a labour, as well as the best Commedy in *Terence* or *Plautus*. And beleeue this, that when hee is gone, and his Commedies out of sale, you will scramble for them, and set vp a new English Inquisition. Take this for a warning, and at the perrill of your pleasures losse, and Iudgements, refuse not, nor like this the lesse, for not being sullied, with the smoaky breath of the multitude; but thanke fortune for the scape it hath made amongst you. Since by the grand possessors wills I beleeue you should haue prayd for them rather then beene prayd. And so I leaue all such to bee prayd for (for the states of their wits healths) that will not praise it. *Vale*.

5. Ben Jonson – (i) *Conversations with William Drummond, 1619.*

His Censure of the English Poets ... That Shaksperr wanted Arte. (Compare 'Censura de Poetis', discussed p. 96).

(ii) Memorial verses contributed to the first Folio (1623). Discussed pp. 16, 35 ff.

To the memory of my beloued,
The AVTHOR
MR. WILLIAM SHAKESPEARE:
AND
what he hath left vs.

To draw no enuy (*Shakespeare*) on thy name,
Am I thus ample to thy Booke, and Fame:

While I confesse thy writings to be such,
　　As neither *Man,* nor *Muse,* can praise too much.
'Tis true, and all mens suffrage. But these wayes
　　Were not the paths I meant vnto thy praise:
For seeliest Ignorance on these may light,
　　Which, when it sounds at best, but eccho's right;
Or blinde Affection, which doth ne're aduance
　　The truth, but gropes, and vrgeth all by chance;
Or crafty Malice, might pretend this praise,
　　And thinke to ruine, where it seem'd to raise.
These are, as some infamous Baud, or Whore,
　　Should praise a Matron. What could hurt her more?
But thou art proofe against them, and indeed
　　Aboue th' ill fortune of them, or the need.
I, therefore will begin. Soule of the Age!
　　The applause! delight! the wonder of our Stage!
My *Shakespeare,* rise; I will not lodge thee by
　　Chaucer, or Spenser, or bid *Beaumont* lye
A little further, to make thee a roome:
　　Thou are a Moniment, without a tombe,
And art aliue still, while thy Booke doth liue,
　　And we haue wits to read, and praise to giue.
That I not mixe thee so, my braine excuses;
　　I meane with great, but disproportion'd *Muses*:
For, if I thought my iudgement were of yeeres,
　　I should commit thee surely with thy peeres,
And tell, how farre thou didstst our *Lily* out-shine,
　　Or sporting *Kid,* or *Marlowes* mighty line.
And though thou hadst small *Latine,* and lesse *Greeke,*
　　From thence to honour thee, I would not seeke
For names; but call forth thund'ring *Aeschilus,*
　　Euripides, and *Sophocles* to vs,
Paccuuius, Accius, him of *Cordoua* dead,
　　To life againe, to heare thy Buskin tread,
And shake a Stage: Or, when thy Sockes were on,
　　Leaue thee alone, for the comparison
Of all, that insolent *Greece,* or haughtie *Rome*
　　sent forth, or since did from their ashes come.
Triumph, my *Britaine,* thou hast one to showe,
　　To whom all Scenes of *Europe* homage owe.
He was not of an age, but for all time!
　　And all the *Muses* still were in their prime,

When like *Apollo* he came forth to warme
   Our eares, or like a *Mercury* to charme!
Nature her selfe was proud of his designes,
   And ioy'd to weare the dressing of his lines!
Which were so richly spun, and wouen so fit,
   As, since, she will vouchsafe no other Wit.
The merry *Greeke*, tart *Aristophanes*,
   Neat *Terence*, witty *Plautus*, now not please;
But antiquated and deserted lye
   As they were not of Natures family.
Yet must I not giue Nature all: Thy Art,
   My gentle *Shakespeare*, must enioy a part.
For though the *Poets* matter, Nature be,
   His Art doth giue the fashion. And, that he,
Who casts to write a liuing line, must sweat,
   (such as thine are) and strike the second heat
Vpon the *Muses* anuile: turne the same,
   (And himselfe with it) that he thinkes to frame;
Or for the lawrell, he may gaine a scorne,
   For a good *Poet's* made, as well as borne.
And such wert thou. Looke how the fathers face
   Liues in his issue, euen so, the race
Of *Shakespeares* minde, and manners brightly shines
   In his well torned, and true-filed lines:
In each of which, he seemes to shake a Lance,
   As brandish't at the eyes of Ignorance.
Sweet Swan of *Auon*! what a sight it were
   To see thee in our waters yet appeare,
And make those flights vpon the bankes of *Thames*,
   That so did take *Eliza*, and our *Iames*!
But stay, I see thee in the *Hemisphere*
   Aduanc'd, and made a Constellation there!
Shine forth, thou Starre of *Poets*, and with rage,
   Or influence, chide, or cheere the drooping Stage;
Which, since thy flight from hence, hath mourn'd like night,
   And despaires day, but for thy Volumes light.

(iii) 'De Shakespeare nostrati', from *Timber: Or Discoveries* (1641). Discussed pp. 96 ff

I remember, the Players have often mentioned it as an honour to *Shakespeare*, that in his writing, (whatsoever he penn'd) hee never blotted out line. My answer hath beene, Would he had blotted a thousand. Which they thought a malevolent speech. I had not told posterity this, but for their ignorance, who choose that circumstance to commend their friend by, wherein he most faulted. And to justifie mine owne candor, (for I lov'd the man, and doe honour his memory (on this side Idolatry) as much as any.) Hee was (indeed) honest, and of an open, and free nature: had an excellent *Phantsie;* brave notions, and gentle expressions: wherein hee flow'd with that facility, that sometime it was necessary he should be stop'd: *Sufflaminandus erat;* as *Augustus* said of *Haterius.* His wit was in his owne power; would the rule of it had beene so too. Many times hee fell into those things, could not escape laughter: As when hee said in the person of *Caesar,* one speaking to him; *Caesar, thou dost me wrong.* Hee replyed: *Caesar did never wrong, but with just cause:* and such like; which were ridiculous. But hee redeemed his vices, with his vertues. There was ever more in him to be praysed, then to be pardoned.

Though Jonson has not lacked annotators, (iii) has been neglected; the Oxford edition, otherwise so helpful, leaves much unexplained. It traces 'De Shakespeare nostrati' to 'our fellow Shakespeare' – 'as he is called in *The Returne from Parnassus'.* The Folio dedication is a more likely source ('so worthy a Friend, & Fellow ... as was our Shakespeare'), but what one really wants to know is how much this not uncommon phrase[2] implied. A very personal relationship? Not necessarily, since it was a traditional way of referring to a classic. Seneca quoted 'our Vergil' ('Vergilius noster', *Epistles,* 70), and Seneca himself was dubbed 'our *Seneca'* by the translator of his *Workes* (1614). By 1612 Spenser was 'our Spencer' (R. M. Cummings, *Spenser The Critical Heritage,* 1971, p. 126); and so on. Again, the Oxford edition did not gloss 'Hee was (indeed) honest' with a reminder that Jonson doted on the word (cf. p. 23). 'On this side Idolatry' needs a cross-reference to Jonson's earlier epigram on Sir William Uvedale's body and soul:

Which (would the world not miscall't flatterie)
I could adore, almost t'idolatrie.

A more ghostly presence in Jonson's paragraph is R. Verstegan's praise of Chaucer in *A Restitution of Decayed Intelligence* (1605):

Geffrey Chaucer . . . is of some called the first illuminator of the English toung: of their opinion I am not (though I reuerence *Chaucer* as an excellent poet for his tyme). He was in deed a great mingler of English with French . . . (p. 203)

Verstegan, writing 'Of the great antiquitie of our ancient English toung', examined the loan-words in English, a feature of the language 'held absurd and friuolous' by some, and the related topics of 'il pro-nountiation' and 'il wryting' (p. 188ff.) Jonson's ideas flow over the same ground: 'il wryting', faults that are absurd, firm disavowal of an esteemed poet, claim that 'I lou'd the man', general assessment starting 'He was indeed . . .'

(iv) Jonson's other allusions to Shakespeare are discussed *passim,* and can be located through the Index.

6. J. Heminge and H. Condell – (i) dedication of the first Folio (1623) to the Earls of Pembroke and Montgomery ('our singular good Lords').

. . . since your L. L. haue beene pleas'd to thinke these trifles some-thing, heeretofore; and haue prosequuted both them, and their Authour liuing, with so much fauour: we hope, that (they out-liuing him, and he not hauing the fate, common with some, to be exequutor to his owne writings) you will vse the like indulgence toward them, you haue done vnto their parent. There is a great difference, whether any Booke choose his Patrones, or finde them: This hath done both. For, so much were your L. L. likings of the seuerall parts, when they were acted, as before they were published, the Volume ask'd to be yours. We haue but collected them, and done an office to the dead, to procure his Orphanes, Guardians; without ambition either of selfe-profit, or fame: onely to keepe the memory of so worthy a Friend, & Fellow aliue, as was our SHAKESPEARE, by humble offer of his playes, to your most noble patronage . . . .

(ii) Epistle to the Readers in the first Folio. Discussed pp. 22, 34, 84.

To the great Variety of Readers.

From the most able, to him that can but spell: There you are number'd.

We had rather you were weighd. Especially, when the fate of all
Bookes depends vpon your capacities: and not of your heads alone, but
of your purses. Well! It is now publique, & you wil stand for your
priuiledges wee know: to read, and censure. Do so, but buy it first.
That doth best commend a Booke, the Stationer saies. Then, how odde
soeuer your braines be, or your wisedomes, make your licence the
same, and spare not. Iudge your sixe-pen'orth, your shillings worth,
your fiue shillings worth at a time, or higher, so you rise to the iust
rates, and welcome. But, what euer you do, Buy. Censure will not
driue a Trade, or make the Iacke go. And though you be a Magistrate
of wit, and sit on the Stage at *Black-Friers,* or the *Cock-pit,* to arraigne
Playes dailie, know, these Playes haue had their triall alreadie, and
stood out all Appeales; and do now come forth quitted rather by a
Decree of Court, then any purchas'd Letters of commendation.

It had bene a thing, we confesse, worthie to haue bene wished, that
the Author himselfe had liu'd to haue set forth, and ouerseen his owne
writings; But since it hath bin ordain'd otherwise, and he by death
departed from that right, we pray you do not envie his Friends, the
office of their care, and paine, to haue collected & publish'd them; and
so to haue publish'd them, as where (before) you were abus'd with
diuerse stolne, and surreptitious copies, maimed, and deformed by the
frauds and stealthes of iniurious impostors, that expos'd them: euen
those, are now offer'd to your view cur'd, and perfect of their limbes;
and all the rest, absolute in their numbers, as he conceiued them.
Who, as he was a happie imitator of Nature, was a most gentle
expresser of it. His mind and hand went together: And what he
thought, he vttered with that easinesse, that wee haue scarce receiued
from him a blot in his papers. But it is not our prouince, who onely
gather his works, and giue them you, to praise him. It is yours that
reade him. And there we hope, to your diuers capacities, you will finde
enough, both to draw, and hold you: for his wit can no more lie hid,
then it could be lost. Reade him, therefore; and againe, and againe:
And if then you doe not like him, surely you are in some manifest
danger, not to vnderstand him. And so we leaue you to other of his
Friends, whom if you need, can bee your guides: if you neede them
not, you can leade you selues, and others. And such Readers we wish
him.

Iohn Heminge
Henrie Condell

7. L. Digges, memorial verses contributed to the first Folio (1623). Discussed p. 38.

TO THE MEMORIE
of the deceased Author Maister
W. SHAKESPEARE.

SHake-speare, at length thy pious fellowes giue
The world thy Workes: thy Workes, by which, out-liue
Thy Tombe, thy name must: when that stone is rent,
And Time dissolues thy *Stratford* Moniment,
Here we aliue shall view thee still. This Booke,
When Brasse and Marble fade, shall make thee looke
Fresh to all Ages: when Posteritie
Shall loath what's new, thinke all is prodegie
That is not *Shake-speares;* eu'ry Line, each Verse
Here shall reuiue, redeeme thee from thy Herse.
Nor Fire, nor cankring Age, as *Naso* said,
Of his, thy wit-fraught Booke shall once inuade.
Nor shall I e're beleeue, or thinke thee dead
(Though mist) vntill our bankrout Stage be sped
(Impossible) with some new straine t'out-do
Passions of *Iuliet,* and her *Romeo;*
Or till I heare a Scene more nobly take,
Then when thy half-Sword parlying *Romans* spake,
Till these, till any of thy Volumes rest
Shall with more fire, more feeling be exprest,
Be sure, our *Shake-speare,* thou canst neuer dye,
But crown'd with Lawrell, liue eternally.

Appendix B

THE 1617 edition of Greene's 'Groats- Worth of Witte'

When *GWW* was reissued in 1617, 'Newly corrected, and of many errors purged', one 'I. H.' added a five-page epistle, addressed 'To Wittie Poets, or Poeticall Wittes', which reads like a general essay on the wits of 1617, triggered off by the autobiographical details of *GWW*. It ridicules the wit that

> makes *Reasons* and *Iudgement,* a payre of false spectacles, where-through to take an imperfect suruey of things *aboue earth;* and so leaping ouer the *Light* of *diuine direction,* falles hudwinckt into the pitfall of its owne Folly: For a *Wit* vnsanctified, is the Diuels *Anuile,* whereon he forges the engines of self-ruine . . .

While Greene is not mentioned by name, this must refer back to his charges against himself in *GWW* – that he had said in his heart 'There is no God', had lived a life of vice and folly, and had brought about his own ruin. What are we to make then of the paragraphs that follow, where I. H. argues that from 'a Wit naturall' (i.e. one unsanctified by divine direction) 'are hatcht these three *vnluckie-Birdes: Impudence, Selfe-conceit, Emulation*'? Again Greene is not named, and yet, in an epistle prefixed to *GWW*, these particular follies are surely picked out because they are strikingly present in Greene's own story. One of the three, Emulation, is chiefly active in Greene's remarks about Shakespeare – so it looks as if I. H. gives Greene his come-uppance for the very sentences that Chettle said he regretted in 1592.

> *Selfe-conceit,* shee prodigiously studies to put out the *Light of wit,* by seeming to know beyond the reach of *Reason,* as if shee had miraculously discouered some stand from off the earth, aboue the sight

130

of *Humanitie,* from whence ouer-looking all, makes it her owne glorie, hypercritically to reproue others.

Emulation, she was nurc't by a shee-Toad; shee neuer lins swelling, till shee burst her selfe, and poysons others . . .

Though it is tempting to see this epistle as another repudiation of *GWW,* and of Greene's letter to the three playwrights, his 'quondam acquaintance', where he hypercritically reproved others, I. H.'s prose and intention remain obscure. The epistle slides into Theophrastan-character writing and, hard though it is to believe, could just have been written by someone unaware that his remarks could be applied to Greene. In a poem also signed by I. H., 'Greenes Epitaph', Greene is called 'Englands second Cicero'. I suspect that I. H. admired Greene's success as a writer and yet felt free to condemn his immoral life. (Greene's popularity as a writer reached a new peak in 1617, when five of his works were issued or reissued, some for the first time in twenty years: *Alcida, Arbasto, Theeves Falling Out, Farewell to Folly, GWW*). The toad that never leaves swelling till she bursts herself is in all probability Greene; and I. H. seems to have thought Greene's reproof of others (including Shakespeare) unjustified – the toad's poison.

Appendix C

The Date of 'The Troublesome Raigne of Iohn King of England.'

It was once taken for granted that *TR*, with its fourteeners and other archaic stylistic features, would have been written some time before it was published in 1591. E. K. Chambers observed that the lines prefixed to Part I, referring to *Tamburlaine*, 'do not claim to be a prologue, and may have been added on publication. The play is not therefore necessarily later than *Tamburlaine* (*c.* 1587). But the tone is that of the Armada period'[1]. The Armada period, of course, began some years before 1588.

We now have new information that was not available to Chambers. (1) Of the many verbal echoes that connect *TR* with *3 Henry VI* and *Richard III* at least one appears to be an echo of Shakespeare by *TR*, since Shakespeare uses words supplied by Holinshed's life of Richard III. (Cf. 'By a divine instinct men's minds mistrust', p. 82, above.) Here the sequence Holinshed → *Richard III* → *TR* is as good as certain, so it is natural to assume a similar one-way traffic where *3 Henry VI* is concerned: Holinshed → *3 Henry VI* → *TR*. Also, *2 Henry VI* preceded *3 Henry VI*, and *1 Henry VI*, whether the first or the last written of the trilogy, is always dated before *Richard III*. Thus, the Shakespearian tetralogy coming between Holinshed (1587) and *TR*, *TR* could scarcely have been written before 1589.

Several smaller points may be added. (2) In *TR*, scene xi, where Faulconbridge seeks 'the Abbots treasure' and finds a nun in the abbot's chest, the 'fat Franciscans' are called 'balde and barefoote *Bungie* birds.' Bullough commented 'Perhaps from "bung", a pickpocket, but there seem to have been Franciscans at Bungay, Suffolk'[2]. Surely, though, with Faulconbridge 'leading a Friar' and the scene purporting so show that friars 'revell so lasciviously', the obvious explanation is that *TR* refers to *Friar Bacon and Friar Bungay* (hereafter *FBB*). In this play Bungay was no doubt presented as a 'shaveling' and bare-foot, like the friars in *TR*; he is 'the jolly friar', suspected of lasciviousness ('I think the friar courts the bonny wench; / Bacon, methinks he is a lusty churl')[3]. *FBB*, not a play marked 'ne' when entered in Henslowe's diary on 19 February 1592, and usually dated 1589–90[4], supports a date of composition for *TR* very close to 1591, its date of publication.

(3) 'Archaic' verse in *TR* need not indicate an early date. For example, the Skeltonical doggerel of the 'friar' scene can be matched in *FBB*, and even later, in Munday and Chettle's Robin Hood plays (1598). Fourteeners are comparatively rare in *TR*, the standard measure being iambic pentameters. (The fourteeners in the 'friar' scene are part of its cultivated quaintness.) More significant than these few hang-overs from earlier drama is the play's extraordinary mish-mash of styles – its different kinds of verse, and also its prose. The verse collapses six separate times into prose in the first scene alone. Such stylistic looseness was exceptional before *The Spanish Tragedy* and *The Old Wive's Tale*, and makes a date before *c.* 1585 unlikely.

(4) *TR* was performed by the Queen's Men, whose most celebrated actor, the clown Richard Tarlton, died in 1588. The absence of an obvious 'Tarlton' role from *TR* points to a date after 1588.

The likelihood that *TR* followed Shakespeare's first tetralogy of history plays, and also *FBB*, gives additional support to the view that *TR* was written not long before it was published in 1591; and this date is consistent with the more substantial argument (cf. pp. 56 ff., 87) that *TR* followed rather than preceded Shakespeare's *King John*.

Notes and References

CHAPTER 1: THE MAN

1 Warren B. Austin has suggested that Chettle, not Greene, wrote *GWW* (*A Computer-Aided Technique for Stylistic Discrimination. The Authorship of 'Greene's Groatsworth of Wit'* (US Dept of Health, Education and Welfare, 1969)). I prefer the older view; the authorship of *GWW*, however, scarcely affects my argument.

2 Harvey, *Works*, I, 72. This is from Harvey's *Fourth Letter*, which he dated 11 and 12 September. If he alludes to the grasshopper in *GWW*, as I think, it would follow that *GWW* was registered late, some time after its publication. (Greene died on 3 September; *GWW* was entered in the SR on 20 September.) The form of the SR entry is also significant ('William wrighte / Entred for his copie . . . / vppon the perill of Henrye Chettle / a booke intituled / GREENES *Groatsworth of wyt*'). Since we know from Chettle's apology that *GWW* was to cause trouble, it looks as if trouble was already anticipated in mid-September: hence the belated SR entry.

3 J. Prime, *The Consolations of David* (1588) A4b.

4 *Caxton's Aesop,* ed. R. T. Lenaghan (Harvard University Press, 1967) pp. 133–4.

5 Alvin B. Kernan thinks that the 'vulgar scandal' was 'sexual in nature' (*The Playwright as Magician* (1979) p. 34). Although sexual 'scandals' are mentioned elsewhere in the sonnets, nos. 110–12 do not point to a sexual theme.

6 See Shakespeare, *The Sonnets,* ed. Hyder Edward Rollins (A New Variorum Edition, 2 vols, 1944) II, 277ff.

7 Compare Sonnet 127: 'For since each hand hath put on nature's power, / *Fairing the foul* with art's false borrow'd face'.

8 *Henslowe Papers,* ed. W. W. Greg (1907) p. 81.

9 Why, we may wonder, would Shakespeare not help an 'old acquaintance'? We know Greene to have been a quarreller; he himself admitted in *GWW* that the number of his own deceits at this time made him 'hatefull almost to all men' (p. 38). It is reasonable to assume that before the actors finally 'forsook' him there were several encounters, involving 'Shake-scene', and bitter words.

10 Since it is sometimes said that John Shakespeare, though bailiff of Stratford, may have been unable to write (because he made his mark in the accounts, and did not sign his name), it is interesting that Sturley, a later bailiff, could switch so easily from English to Latin. The fact that Sturley got the tag from Virgil wrong ('hoc opus, hic labor est', *Aeneid,* vi. 129) also suggests that Latin came easily to him.

11 Either as lender or, perhaps, as broker.

12 EKC, II, 113–18.

13 *Ratseis Ghost* (1605) B1a–B1b (Shakespeare Association Facsimiles, No. 10, 1935).

14 EKC, *ES,* II, 215.

15 G. L. Hosking, *The Life and Times of Edward Alleyn* (1952) p. 17.

16 EKC, *ES* ii, 298. Hosking (p. 144) says that Alleyn 'began negotiations' for the Dulwich purchase in the summer of 1605.
17 Hosking, pp. 122, 147.
18 EKC, i, 84.
19 See A. M. Nagler, *Shakespeare's Stage* (New Haven, 1958) p. 75ff.
20 Hosking, p. 143.
21 See William Ingram, *A London Life in the Brazen Age Francis Langley 1548–1602* (1978) p. 145.
22 W. Ingram, ibid.
23 By W. Ingram (see n. 21).
24 See p. 8, above.
25 EKC, ii, 113–18.
26 EKC, ii, 140.
27 EKC, i, 75.
28 Quoted EKC, ii, 100.
29 E. R. C. Brinkworth, *Shakespeare and the Bawdy Court of Stratford* (1972) p. 80.
30 In Bradley's *Oxford Lectures on Poetry* (1909). I quote from the 1950 edition.
31 Bradley, p. 325.
32 Bradley, p. 319.
33 EKC, ii, 194, 195.
34 C. Ockland, *Elizabeth Queene* (1585) D1b.
35 R. M. Cummings, *Spenser The Critical Heritage* (1971) p.116.
36 EKC, ii, 266, 267.
37 Schoenbaum, *Life*, 205.
38 A. Harbage recently revived the theory that Spenser's allusion in *Teares of the Muses* (1591) to 'Our pleasant *Willy*' ('that same gentle Spirit, from whose pen / Large streames of honnie and sweete Nectar flowe') is to Shakespeare (*PQ*, xli (1962) 18–36). Chambers felt that the 'date is too early to make a reference to Sh. ... at all plausible' (ii, 186). I cannot agree with Chambers' reason, but think it unlikely that Sp. would praise Sh. in this poem, which laments the decay of learning: Sh. did not strike contemporaries as a man of learning. Sp.'s later tribute to Aetion ('A gentler shepheard may no where be found' (EKC, ii, 187)) could refer to Sh. or to Drayton; we should keep in mind, though, that Sp. used 'gentle' freely. The nearest thing to an open reference to 'gentle' Sh. before 1616 occurs in J. Davies, *Microcosmos* (1603): 'And though the *stage* doth staine pure gentle *bloud*, / Yet generous yee are in *minde* and *moode*' (in margin: 'W.S. R. B.'; EKC, ii, 213). But here *gentle* means *generosus*, well-born, not 'sweet-natured.'
39 Cf. Alvin B. Kernan, *The Playwright as Magician* (1979) ch. I.
40 Cf. *Shepheards Calender*, December, 1; *Faerie Queene*, VI, x, xxix; *Astrophel*, 1, etc.
41 Jonson, viii, 50, 99, 229.
42 Ibid., 82, 216.
43 See p. 93.
44 Although *gentle* was a richer word in Sh.'s time, I suspect that Sh. might have shared Lamb's irritation had he known that he would be called 'gentle': 'For God's sake ... don't make me ridiculous any more by terming me gentle-hearted ... the meaning of "gentle" is equivocal at best, and almost always means poor-spirited' (*The Letters of Charles Lamb*, ed. A. Ainger, 2 vols, 1891, i, 121–2). Compare also Herbert Howarth, 'Shakespeare's Gentleness' (*Sh. Survey 14* (1961) 90–97).
45 A. Scoloker, *Daiphantus* (quoted from E. Arber, *An English Garner*, vol. vii (1883).

46 EKC, ii, 197.
47 EKC, ii, 252.
48 Quoted from *The Poems of William Barksted,* ed. A. B. Grosart (privately printed, 1876).
49 See Schoenbaum, *Life,* 205.
50 Sonnets 40, 42.
51 EKC, ii, 205. It is difficult to see who could be meant by 'some better natures' if not Shakespeare.
52 See pp. 109–20.
53 EKC, ii, 213–14; see also above, ch. I, n.38.
54 For Chettle, see p. 121; for Jaggard, EKC, i. 547.
55 Cf. p. 49.
56 Jonson, i, 150.
57 *Ibid.,* i, 140, 145.
58 Cf. p. 21.
59 EKC, ii, 252 (Aubrey), 249 (Ward), 245 (Fuller). Edward Wagenknecht went too far, I think, in arguing that Shakespeare 'held himself aloof' and that, 'except as a business man and a Stratfordian, he never belonged to a group' (*The Personality of Shakespeare* (Norman, Oklahoma, 1972) pp. 138, 141). Shakespeare's 'group' was, surely, the company of actors to which he belonged; Augustine Phillips' bequests to his fellows (EKC, ii, 73), and Shakespeare's later, indicate that the company was bound together by more than legal ties. And, though most of the sharers were actors, not writers, the company must have had its literary preferences, if not a defined literary policy, and would thus have impressed contemporaries as a powerful group in the literary world.

CHAPTER 2: THE WRITER

1   E. Malone, *Shakespeare* (1821, 21 vols.), xviii, 571.
2   Cf. E. Honigmann, *MLR* (1954), xlix, 293–307; Schoenbaum, *Life,* 116.
3   Nashe, iii, 312, 315.
4   Cf. p. 72.
5   Compare *OED,* factotum; also G. W., *The Censure of a loyall Subiect* (1587), 'the *Spaniard* will be *Domine, fac totum,* wheresoeuer he ruleth' (F2b); J. Florio, *Second Frutes* (1591), 'like a Dictator he is *Dominus fac totum*' (Y4); G. Harvey, *Pierces Supererogation* (1593), in *Works,* ii, 208.
6   Compare also *Willobie his Avisa* (1594), where the author's 'familiar friend W. S.' may be Shakespeare; and L. Hotson's discussion in *I, William Shakespeare* (1937), ch. iii.
7   Bentley, *Profession of Dramatist,* p. 60.
8   Cf. EKC, ii, 188, 319ff.; also G. Ungerer, 'An Unrecorded Elizabethan Performance of *Titus Andronicus*' (*Sh. S.,* 14 (1961) 102–9); G. Tillotson, *Essays in Criticism and Research* (Cambridge, 1942) pp. 41–48, for the 1610 production of *Othello.*
9   Nashe, *Works,* iii, 316; *GWW,* Fla.
10 Harvey, *Works,* ii, 215.
11 The two early 'tributes' are to *1 Henry vi* and *Comedy of Errors* (see note 8, above). Nashe's reference to 'braue *Talbot*' in *Pierce Penilesse* (1592) is generally thought to refer to *1 Henry vi*; since Nashe and Greene were quarrelling with Shakespeare at this

time, it is possible that Nashe did not connect Shakespeare with the play.

12 Since the publication of the *Allusion-Book* of 1932, some additional allusions have been discovered (e.g. by Bentley, in *Shakespeare & Jonson*).

13 II, V, XV, etc.

14 Bentley, *Shakespeare & Jonson,* II, 10.

15 Cf. p. 37.

16 Pistol's 'title-page' career is of special interest. He is named on the quarto title-page of each of the three plays in which he appears. The first was probably *Henry V* (SR 4 August 1600), quoted p. 33. Here Pistol may be named because the same printer, T. Creede, had printed 'The Famous Victories of Henry the fifth: Containing the Honourable Battle of Agin-court ... 1598'; Pistol thus helped to distinguish the two plays. Creede also printed *2 Henry IV* and *Merry Wives.* Since different publishers brought out the three Pistol plays it may be that the printer devised the blurbs. If so, Creede's instinct was sound, for other allusions prove Pistol to have been a favourite (*Allusion-Book,* I, 90, 151, 190, 197).

17 EKC, II, 200.

18 *Sh. Survey, 4* (1951) p. 83.

19 See G. Tillotson in ftn. 8, above.

20 It has been suggested that Jonson acted as 'editor' of the first Folio, or as Heminge and Condell's helper when the Folio's preliminary matter was put together. (See W. W. Greg, *The Shakespeare First Folio* (Oxford, 1955) pp. 3–4, 18, 78–9; E. Honigmann, *The Stability of Shakespeare's Text* (1965) p. 34).

21 Jonson's thoughts about *J. C., Macbeth* and *Pericles* were recorded after 1623, but I assume that he did not make a secret of them.

22 Appendix A, p. 126.

23 About two years after the Folio was published with a title that studiously avoided the word 'Works', Richard James reported that 'A young Gentle lady ... having read ye works of Shakespeare, made me this question ...' (EKC, II, 241)!

24 E. Honigmann, *op. cit.,* 34–35.

25 Greg, *op. cit.,* p. 450.

26 *Shakespeare & Jonson,* I, 107.

27 *Op. cit.,* I, 11.

28 D. L. Frost, *The School of Shakespeare* (Cambridge, 1968) p. 20. I am indebted to Frost's useful book throughout this chapter, but disagree with some of his opinions.

29 W. W. Greg, 'Shakespeare and Jonson', *RES,* XXII, (1946) 58.

30 Bentley, I, 58.

31 Bentley, I, 112.

32 Bentley, I, 111, 109.

33 C. C. H. Williamson, *Readings on the Character of Hamlet* (1950) p. 5.

34 Williamson, *op cit.,* p. 4.

35 For Scoloker see also p. 18.

36 G. E. Bentley, *Shakespeare A Biographical Handbook* (New Haven, 1961) p. 203.

37 Bentley, *op. cit.,* p. 170.

38 Dryden, *Essays,* I, 80.

39 See p. 71, below.

40 *RES* XIV, (1938) 20–43.

41 See Greg, *The Shakespeare First Folio,* pp. 11–17.

42 See the edition of the play by W. A. Abrams (Durham, N.C., 1942).

43 Greg, *op. cit.,* p. 375ff.

44 EKC, I, 84, 86.
45 In one of the 'Shakespeare novels' there is another clue suggesting that the printer or publisher behaved in an unusual way. The normal running-title in Wilkins' *Pericles* novel is 'A patterne of the painefull Aduentures / of Pericles Prince of Tyre'; on A4b and B1a it is '*The Patterne* / of Pericles Prince of Tyre' – and is clearly lifted from Wilkins' source, L. Twine's version of the Apollonius story, where the running-title was '*The Patterne* / *of painfull Aduentures*' (ed.? 1594). The author would not normally be concerned with a book's running-titles; it looks as if Wilkins gave a copy of Twine to his printer (and this may help to explain why there are passages in Wilkins' novel that are almost identical with Twine). See my review in *Sh. Q.*, VI, (1955) 98–100.
46 Bentley, *Profession of Dramatist*, p. 280.
47 *The Stability of Shakespeare's Text*, pp. 172–92.
48 'The Elizabethan Printer and Dramatic Manuscripts' (*The Library*, XII, (1931) 253–75).
49 Marlowe (*Edward II, Dido*), Chapman (*Blind Beggar*).
50 F. Meres, *Palladis Tamia* (1598), sig. 206b ff.
51 See Schoenbaum, *Life*, pp. 171–2.
52 EKC, I, 550.

CHAPTER 3: SHAKESPEARE'S FIRST PLAYS

1 For a different explanation of R. B.'s stanza see W. B. Austin, *Sh. Q.*, VI, (1955) 373ff.
2 EKC, I, 270.
3 F. P. Wilson, *Marlowe and the Early Shakespeare* (Oxford, 1953) p. 113.
4 See Peter Alexander, *Shakespeare's 'Henry VI' and 'Richard III'* (Cambridge, 1929) 201ff., and *Shakespeare* (Home Univ. Lib., 1964) 167ff.
5 T. M. Parrott in *JEGP* LV, (1956) 297–305; cf. R. A. Law in *SP*, LIV (1957) 119–27; K. Muir, 'Source Problems in the Histories' (*Shakespeare Jahrbuch* (Heidelberg, 1960) vol. 96).
6 *TR* and *True Tragedie* were assigned to the Queen's Men on their title-pages. For *A Shrew*, see Honigmann, 'Shakespeare's "Lost Source-Plays"' (*MLR*, 1954, XLIX, 306–7), and also G. M. Pinciss in *Sh. Survey* 27 (1974) 129–36.
7 K. Muir, 'Source Problems', p. 50.
8 See W. W. Greg, '*The Spanish Tragedy* – A Leading Case?', *The Library*, VI, (1926) 53.
9 K. Muir, *The Sources of Shakespeare's Plays* (1977) p. 79.
10 *King John*, ed. R. L. Smallwood, (New Penguin Shakespeare, 1974) p. 367.
11 Muir, *Sources*, p. 163. Compare also W. H. Matchett's answer to the 'obscurity' charge in his Signet edition of *King John*, p. 154.
12 Alice Walker, *RES*, VII, (1956) 421–3.
13 See Holinshed's *Chronicles* (1587 ed.), vol. 3, pp. 118 etc., 197 (for W. Marshall), pp. 159, 162 (for G. FitzPeter).
14 In Act V Salisbury displaces Pembroke as the earl named first in stage directions in *King John*, presumably because of his leading role in the rebellion against John.
15 See W. W. Greg, *The Shakespeare First Folio* (Oxford, 1955), pp. 177, 184; A. S. Cairncross, 'Quarto Copy for Folio *Henry V*' (*SB* VIII, 1956, 67–93).
16 See Greg, p. 60.

17 See the following editions of *King John*: New Cambridge (1936), p. xlv ff.; New Arden (1954), p. xxxvi ff.; Signet (1966), p. 148ff.; New Penguin (1974), pp. 354, 373.

18 Parrott, *loc. cit.,* p. 301.

19 Greg, *op. cit.,* p. 110.

20 Muir, 'Source Problems in the Histories', p. 50; *Sources,* p. 58ff., 78ff.

21 R. Greene, *The Spanish Masquerado* (1589) B4a, E3b; D. F. R. de M., *An Answer to the Untruthes Published and Printed in Spaine* (1589); *Locrine* (*c.* 1590) (in *Apocrypha,* p. 44); T. Nashe, *Works,* I, 185, and II, 114. My italics. See also Greene, *Friar Bacon* (1594) C1b, and Peele, *Alcazar* (1594) C4b, D1a.

22 I. L., *The Birth, Purpose, and mortall Wound of the Romish Holie League* (1589) A2b.

23 R. W., *The Three Lords and Three Ladies of London* (1590) G3a, G4a.

24 See S. Daniel, *The Civil Wars,* ed. Laurence Michel (New Haven, 1958) p. 347.

25 George M. Logan (*Shakespeare Studies,* IX, 1976, 121–40) argues that Shakespeare's *Richard II* resembles Daniel's *Civil Wars* at points where Daniel follows Lucan, and concludes that *Civil Wars* (1595) preceded *Richard II.* Such a view is not incompatible with my date for *King John,* even though *KJ* and *Richard II* are often dated close together: the internal evidence for dating Shakespeare's early plays tells us little about their precise order (cf. also p. 85.)

26 M. P. McDiarmid in *Notes and Queries,* (October, 1957) 435ff.

27 Holinshed, vol. 3, p. 319.

28 Holinshed, vol. 3, p. 69.

29 See Charles Knight, *Studies of Shakspere* (1849); Thomas Kenny, *The Life and Genius of Shakespeare* (1864); Peter Alexander, *Shakespeare's 'Henry VI and 'Richard III'* (Cambridge, 1929) p. 200ff.

30 Jonson, VI, 16.

31 Jonson, IV, 41.

32 EKC, I, 345.

33 *Romeo and Juliet,* ed. G. I. Duthie (New Cambridge ed., 1955) p. xvi.

34 Sidney Thomas, *MLN,* LXIV, (1949), 417–19.

35 EKC, I, 270.

36 G. Harvey, *Works,* II, 91; *Love's Labour's Lost,* IV. 2. 79ff.

37 See Nashe, *Works,* I, 154; Harvey, *Works,* II, 75. Shakespeare may have been more suspicious than others about Nashe and *GWW* if he noticed that the attack on 'Shakescene' closely resembled parts of the epistle to Greene's *Menaphon* (1589), which was signed by Nashe (see *MLR* XLIX, (1954), 294). He may also have thought that Nashe was throwing his weight around too much on the literary scene, for, in addition to his acknowledged satires, Nashe was believed to be the author of an epistle in Munday's *Gerileon,* Part 2 (1592) where 'T. N.' lashed various literary enemies. Chettle later explained that he, not Nashe, wrote this epistle, 'though by the workmans error T. N. were set to the end' (*Kind-Harts Dreame,* A4a). Shakespeare's riposte in *LLL* is, I think, good-humoured: he mocks the impudence of the young satirist who feels he knows better than his elders ('well-educated infant', 'Thou disputes like an infant', I. 2. 90, V. 1. 57), puns on his nick-name, perhaps hints that he suspects him of having had a hand in *GWW* ('thou half-penny purse of wit', V. 1. 63).

38 See no. 3, above.

CHAPTER 4: SHAKESPEARE'S FIRST PLAYS (*contd*)

1 See p. 56.
2 Schoenbaum, *Life*, ch. 10; and *Shakespeare's Lives* (Oxford, 1970) p. 704.
3 Chambers, *ES*, II, 130.
4 Kenneth Muir, *Sources*, p. 19.
5 *The Taming of the Shrew*, ed. G. R. Hibbard (New Penguin Shakespeare, 1968) p. 42; *The Taming of the Shrew*, ed. B. R. Morris (New Arden Shakespeare, 1981) Introduction.
6 See p. 25, above, and EKC, I, 59.
7 See *MLR* XLIX, (1954) 295.
8 *The Plays and Poems of William Shakespeare*, ed. E. Malone (21 vols, 1821) II, 315.
9 EKC, II, 226.
10 EKC, I, 55.
11 *The Third Part of King Henry VI*, ed. A. S. Cairncross (New Arden Shakespeare, 1964) p. xliv.
12 A. C. Judson, *The Life of Edmund Spenser* (Baltimore, 1945) p. 127.
13 EKC, I, 402, 244.
14 D. C. Allen, *Francis Meres's Treatise 'Poetrie' A Critical Edition* (University of Illinois Studies in Language and Literature, vol. XVI; Urbana, 1933) pp. 31, 55.
15 Cf. p. 51.
16 EKC, I, 320.
17 Chambers in *TLS*, 28 August, 1930.
18 *Othello*, ed. Alice Walker and J. Dover Wilson (New Cambridge Shakespeare, 1957), p. xv.
19 H. Dugdale Sykes, *Sidelights on Shakespeare* (1919) p. 99ff.
20 Rupert Taylor, *PMLA*, LI, (1936) 633ff.
21 For Cairncross see n. 11, above; Holinshed, *Chronicles* (1587, vol. 3), p. 721; *Richard III*, II. 3. 37–44.
22 See p. 71.
23 EKC, I, 140; W. W. Greg, *The Shakespeare First Folio* (Oxford, 1955) p. 60.
24 See p. 71.
25 F. P. Wilson, quoted p. 56.
26 E. M. W. Tillyard, *Shakespeare's History Plays* (Penguin Books, 1962 ed.) p. 216.
27 See K. Muir, *Shakespeare's Comic Sequence* (1979) p. 15.
28 Chambers, *ES*, II, 104.
29 Chambers, *ES*, II, 111; *Henslowe's Diary*, ed. R. A. Foakes and R. T. Rickert (Cambridge, 1961) p. 7.
30 Chambers, *ES*, II, 112, 114; W. W. Greg, *Two Elizabethan Stage Abridgements: The Battle of Alcazar & Orlando Furioso* (Oxford, 1923).
31 As in n. 30, above.
32 I am aware that it has been reaffirmed that Shakespeare was himself one of the Queen's Men: see G. M. Pinciss, as in ch. III, n. 6.
33 See pp. 66–9, 82–3.
34 EKC, II, 254.
35 EKC, II, 264.
36 Leslie Hotson, *Shakespeare's Sonnets Dated and other Essays* (1949) p. 232.
37 For the 'vpstart Crow' see p. 25. As for Chettle, I disbelieve that 'qualitie' means the acting profession, since Chettle (see Appendix A, p. 121) paraphrases his remarks in

what follows. He apologises for two of Greene's allegations (financial ruthlessness; professional incompetence, since Greene claimed that Shake-scene bombasts out blank verses), saying that he himself and 'diuers of worship' testify to the contrary; 'vprightnes of dealing' therefore repeats 'ciuill demeanor', and 'his facetious grace in writting' repeats 'exelent in the qualitie he professes.' Chettle thought of Shakespeare as primarily a writer, not an actor.

CHAPTER 5: CONTEMPORARY CRITICISMS OF SHAKESPEARE

1 EKC, II, 211.
2 Dryden, *Essays,* I, 203, 224.
3 'Huffing' seems to have meant 'ranting'. Compare also N. Breton (1603): 'it is not your huftie tuftie can make mee afraid of your bigge lookes: for I saw the Play of Ancient Pistoll, where a Cracking Coward was well cudgeld ... your railing is so neare the Rascall' (*Allusion-Book*, I, 90).
4 Nashe, III, 311.
5 Cf. Honigmann, *MLR,* (1954) XLIX, 294.
6 Nashe, I, 195.
7 Jonson, VII, 587.
8 E. Bolton urged in 1610 that writers should 'have a singuler care' of 'language & style'; though English lacks rules for 'true writing', and 'fewe there be who have the most proper graces thereof', there are some books 'out of which wee gather the most warrantable English'. Bolton's list included 'Shakespere' (*Allusion-Book*, I, 213).
9 Dryden, *Essays,* I, 80, 81.
10 S. Gosson, *Playes Confuted* (1582) quoted from EKC, *ES,* IV, 215; Sidney, *An Apology for Poetry*, ed. G. Shepherd (1965) p. 134.
11 Jonson, of course, echoed Quintilian and other classical authors in some of these passages: see the Commentary on *Discoveries* in the Oxford *Ben Jonson.*
12 *The Alchemist*, ed. F. H. Mares (The Revels Plays, 1967) p. 5.
13 Cf. also EKC, II, 247; *Volpone*, prologue.
14 See *John Webster*, ed. G. K. and S. K. Hunter (Penguin Critical Anthologies, 1969) p. 30.
15 Jonson, III, 515.
16 Jonson, III, 467.
17 See *The Sonnets*, ed. Hyder E. Rollins (A New Variorum Edition, 2 vols, 1944) II, 283.
18 EKC, II, 245.
19 Schoenbaum, *Life*, p. 207.
20 I. A. Shapiro, *MLR,* XLVI, (1951) 63.
21 EKC, II, 243.
22 Greene, the only other contemporary rival we know of, elicited a less humble response from Shakespeare, and the style of his hasty compositions could scarcely be described as 'precious phrase by all the Muses fil'd' (Sonnet 85). The other allusions in Sonnets 78—86 do not point to Greene, though I have suggested (p. 6) that *o'ergreen* in Sonnet 112 may refer to him.
23 Compare T. Plume's note (mid-seventeenth century): 'Here lies Ben Johnson – who

was once one – (this he made of himself – Shakspear took the pen from him & made this) Here lies Benjamin – with short hair upon his Chin – / Who while he lived was a slow thing – & now he's buried is no thing' (EKC II, 247; I have added brackets, changed italics).

24 I assume that the dedicatee was not the 'only begetter' of all the sonnets. Some of the 'Dark Lady' sonnets have nothing to do with him, and there are other sonnets that point to a different begetter. Andrew Gurr has made the intriguing suggestion that No. 145 puns on 'hate away' – Hathaway (*Essays in Criticism* (1971), XXI, 221–6). I think that other sonnets included in the 'Young Man' sequence may have been addressed to Anne Hathaway or another lady (e.g. No. 109), and that more than one patron may be involved (cf. p. 7): the sonnets for 'W. H.' could have formed one section of the MS., followed by others written in the same style but intended for different recipients.

25 Schoenbaum, *Life,* 151, 258.

26 Cf. pp. 124, 126.

27 For Jonson and Shakespeare see also S. Schoenbaum, 'Shakespeare and Jonson: Fact and Myth' (*The Elizabethan Theatre II*. Papers given at the University of Waterloo, 1969 (1970) pp. 1–19.)

CHAPTER 6: SHAKESPEARE'S REPLY TO CRITICISM

1 Jonson, I, 151.

2 Jonson, I, 145.

3 Jonson, I, 141, 151.

4 See pp. 93 ff.

5 E. Honigmann, 'Shakespeare's "bombast"' (in *Shakespeare's Styles: Essays in honour of Kenneth Muir,* ed. Philip Edwards etc., (1980) pp. 151–62).

6 See p. 95. See also Harriet Hawkins, *Likenesses of Truth in Elizabethan and Restoration Drama* (Oxford, 1972).

7 J. Keats, *Letters* (22 November, 1817).

8 Claudian, *The Rape of Proserpine,* tr. L. Digges (1617).

APPENDIX A

1 What had Chettle in mind when he referred to Shakespeare's 'facetious' grace in writing? *OED* cites Chettle as the only entry for 'facetious, 1': '[After L. *facetus.*] Of style, manners, etc.: Polished and agreeable, urbane.' It is interesting that Nashe wrote in 1589 that in a discussion of 'the seuerall qualities required in *Castalions* Courtier', one man upheld 'the necessitie of that affabilitie, which our Latinists entitle *facetus,* & we more familiarlie describe by the name of discoursing' (Nashe, *Works,* I, 7). *OED* explains 'affability' as 'The quality of being affable; readiness to converse or be addressed – especially by inferiors or equals; courteousness, civility, openness of manner.' While Chettle's 'facetious' could have been intended as 'polished' etc., Nashe's gloss suggests that Chettle's word was the first tribute to Shakespeare's ready tongue and pen – anticipating 'what he thought, he vttered with that easinesse, that wee haue scarce receiued from him a blot in his papers' (cf. p. 128, above). I would gloss 'facetious' as 'easy.'

2 Lat. *nostras, nostratis,* meant 'of our country', and that seems to be what L. Digges meant in a letter of *c.* 1613 — 'this Booke of Sonets, which with Spaniards here is accounted of their lope de Vega as in Englande wee sholde our Will Shakespeare' (P. Morgan, *Sh. Survey 16,* (1963) p. 118).

APPENDIX C

1 EKC, *EC* IV, 23–4.
2 G. Bullough, *Narrative and Dramatic Sources of Shakespeare* (8 vols, 1957 etc.) IV, 104.
3 II. 3. 175, II. 3. 40.
4 See *Friar Bacon and Friar Bungay,* ed. J. A. Lavin (The New Mermaids, 1969) p. xiii.

Index